# The Gravy

Dr. John's freezer contains two small squirrels, a back strap from a small white-tailed doe, an elk roast, ground meat from a sacred ceremony, a duck, homegrown shallots, chickpeas, and chicken feet.

# The Gravy

*In the Kitchen with*
*New Orleans Musicians*

Elsa Hahne

High ISO Music / *New Orleans*

Design by Elsa Hahne
Printed in China

ISBN 978-0-9883960-0-5 (cloth : alk. paper)

Library of Congress Control Number:  2012917914
1. Cookery, American—Louisiana style. 2. Cookery—
Louisiana—New Orleans. 3. Food habits—Louisiana—
New Orleans. 4. Cookery, International.

Published by High ISO Music
New Orleans, LA
info@highisomusic.com
www.highisomusic.com

To order this book online, visit
www.highisomusic.com, or www.offbeat.com.
To get updates on *The Gravy*, as well as on *You Are Where
You Eat* (Elsa Hahne's previous book), become a fan at
www.facebook.com/YouAreWhereYouEat.

To Golden

Theresa Andersson recorded her last two albums in her house, mainly in her kitchen.

# Contents

# foreword

I've been collecting recipes and cookbooks since I was a teenager. I would sit for hours cutting out recipes and pasting them into a massive binder. I started collecting cookbooks because I thought that food was one of the more interesting manifestations of a culture. If you know what and how people eat, then you can really understand where they're coming from.

One of the first cookbooks I ever bought was the series of *Time-Life* cookbooks, *Foods of the World*. I have the whole series, and I've probably read those books a million times. I loved them. It was kind of an introduction to the world for me; places I'd never been, places I wanted to go. One recipe I cooked a lot from those books was beef Stroganoff. I followed it to the letter. I'd made plans to go to Russia, and I took Russian in college—you do crazy things when you're in your twenties. Of course, I never made it to Russia, but I cooked beef Stroganoff a lot.

In New Orleans, everyone has their own way of cooking everything, which is one of the things people always talk about here—food. I don't care who you meet, I don't care where you are, all you have to do is mention food and people will start talking about their different recipes, how they make it, how they don't like it there, and how it's better here. New Orleans are obsessed with food.

To New Orleanians, music and food mean home— whether people realize it or not. Some people who move away from New Orleans become aware of that pretty quickly. But a lot of people who live here take it for granted, which is why *OffBeat* was born 25 years ago—to raise the awareness of people who aren't necessarily music people to the importance of music in our culture.

When Elsa Hahne and I first started working together at *OffBeat*, I wasn't aware that she had written a cookbook (*You Are Where You Eat*—highly recommended!). Elsa's talent as a writer, photographer, and designer, and her passion for local cuisine, was just the ingredient we needed to develop a monthly series in *OffBeat* called "The Gravy," which is the basis for this book. Elsa has stirred some more roux into "The Gravy" and has created a cookbook that captures New Orleans' finest music and food.

So here, in all its glossy glory, is a cookbook for music and food lovers alike: *The Gravy*. Enjoy!

—*Jan Ramsey, publisher of* OffBeat *magazine*

*To become a monthly subscriber to* OffBeat *magazine, no matter where you live, visit www.offbeat.com/subscriptions.*

# Preface

Creativity rarely limits itself to one area in life, and given time and means, creative people have a tendency to branch out.

In New Orleans, musicians can often make a living as musicians because of the relatively low cost of housing and the number of clubs that offer live music every night. Musicians also take on a variety of side jobs—often involving food. A valuable part of the local economy is based on what started as culinary hobbies. Guitarist Brint Anderson studied cooking at Delgado; bounce artist 10th Ward Buck opened his own chicken wing establishment on Jackson Avenue; DJ Captain Charles has been involved with many different restaurants over the years; Antoinette K-Doe fed her community at the Mother-in-Law Lounge before she passed away; and singer Sophie Lee opened her own club, Three Muses, on Frenchmen Street, where her grandmother's Korean Boolgogi Rice Bowl remains a fixture on the menu.

This book started out as a monthly series in *OffBeat*, New Orleans' premier music magazine, which has been around since 1988. I have been the art director at the magazine since 2008, when my first book, *You Are Where You Eat—Stories and Recipes from the Neighborhoods of New Orleans* (University Press of Mississippi), came out. That book focused on home cooks from all around the city telling their own stories and sharing some of their favorite recipes through first-person accounts. When Jan Ramsey, the publisher and motor-mama of *OffBeat*, and I started talking about different projects we could do together, the idea of a musicians' cooking series in the magazine led to a phone call to Irma Thomas, who used to cook red beans and rice for the audience at the Lion's Den, her R&B club on Gravier Street, which was destroyed by Hurricane Katrina in 2005. Irma wasn't shy; she'd talked up her recipe for macaroni and cheese before, and didn't mind sharing it with *OffBeat* readers in our September 2008 issue. After Irma, the project ran away with me. I didn't exactly have any trouble finding other musicians who could cook, and four years later, the series is still going.

The connection between music and food is magic, not mystery, in New Orleans. Restaurants continue to add live music to their menus, while music clubs increasingly make efforts to let people hear about their food. Music and food are such a large part of New Orleans culture that it's hard to have one without the other—not sure why one should. Playing and cooking skills are passed down from generation to generation, from neighbor to neighbor, musician to musician. All rely on a sense of tradition and improvisation, balance and bravado, excellent timing, as well as a desire to communicate and please.

Most of the material in this book comes straight from the *OffBeat* magazine series, with some important additions.

I wanted to include food photography of all the recipes, as well as photos of the musicians' instruments, and photos of the musicians performing their music. I've also included a quick bio for each person, the same way I did for *You Are Where You Eat*, including each person's "holy trinity" of ingredients.

Traditionally, the holy trinity consists of onion, bell pepper, and celery—with the minor trio (garlic, green onions, and parsley) as backup singers. The holy trinities in this book are the three key ingredients each musician uses the most in his or her kitchen. I've also included a song—one notable recording—as an introduction to their music. Most of the musicians in this book perform in and around New Orleans on a regular basis, so please—eat up, listen up, and join the party.

—*Elsa Hahne*

*Author's note: I do not recommend or guarantee all the different ingredients and cooking methods in this book. Each musician gives his or her own opinion. Please leave roadkill by the roadside. And be careful where you get your raccoons.*

# Acknowledgements

This book is a testament to the creativity, tenacity, and diversity of New Orleans' music community. It would not exist without the passion and persistence of New Orleans musicians and music fans, Louisiana food lovers, and all the people who have made an uncompromising commitment to enjoy themselves and share their talent.

Special thanks go out to the staff at *OffBeat* magazine, Bethany Bultman and the New Orleans Musicians' Clinic, Zatarain's, Rob Schauffler of Forest Sales, Cameron Wood, Judy Walker of the *Times-Picayune*, Amy Kirk and the French Market, Cassady Fallon Cooper, Heather Price Cooper, Rebecca Snedeker, University Press of Mississippi (publisher of my first book, *You Are Where You Eat—Stories and Recipes from the Neighborhoods of New Orleans*), as well as to my partner, Golden G. Richard, III.

This book was made possible through grants from the Threadhead Cultural Foundation, as well as the New Orleans Jazz & Heritage Festival and Foundation, Inc.

# Introduction
## by Dr. John

We [musicians] all kind of got stuck in this thing, in cooking, because we like certain things. I used to sit on the back of the band bus and we'd be talking about how we liked this and that cooked this and that way. We used to sit on the back of the bus and talk about food forever. But that's what a lot of musicians do. We're going to have to cook certain things the way we like them. Ain't nobody going to cook it the way I've got to cook something today.

I learned to cook from hanging around my Aunt Gueneri. But also I watched my pa. My mama would never cook squirrels. But my pa would say, "I've got squabs tonight!" And she'd cook them because she didn't know they was pigeons. He'd take my BB gun and shoot pigeons off the roof of his shop, and have a bunch of pigeons and call them squab, and that was food, and it was good. But she would not cook them squirrels, so my pa would cook them. And I watched him cook. My Aunt Gueneri also cooked a great Sicilian dish with rabbit. It was so hip. Wild rabbits. We used to always take them over to my Uncle Junior who was squatting in the west of the Bonnet Carré Spillway. He'd just fatten them up a little bit with all that stuff that was around his pad. Back then, there was no tons of water there. It was just where people squatted. He'd never worn shoes since World War II.

Squirrel sauce piquant is delicious. But see, I can't eat that now. I had to shift all my gears. If I eat something that's fried, I eat it with buckwheat flour. I can't eat just regulation flour. But a lot of people don't want to cook with that. I can deal with it, but some other people don't want to deal with that—they'd rather have corn meal, but I can't have corn. A lot of stuff, I can't have today. I didn't know how bad all this stuff was, like shellfish and dairy products, for your liver. I didn't know how bad 'til I had cirrhosis of the liver number four and it looked like multi-colored Jello. The biopsy, when they take a chunk of liver out, it looked like purple, yellow, and red Jello. Didn't even look like a liver! But that's when you're in bad stages of cirrhosis. I got past it by dealing with other ways of hooking up. If I cook a squirrel or something today, I try to stuff him up with a sweet potato, just little bits of somethings, because they're small critters. But I love to eat. My favorite thing with squirrels is eating squirrel brains. I like to crack them heads open and just chew on the brains. It's like a delicacy to me. But there's a million ways to cook that. Wallace [Boudreaux who lives with Dr. John and cooks most of the time] would cook them totally different than me. That's what we do here. Everybody got their own way of hooking everything and anything up.

Wallace goes back in my life to a long, long time ago, probably when he was a real youngster, even no teenager yet. Him and a bunch of my cousins would hang out. We was all participating in illegal activities, but we had a good time. If you can put things in perspectives, I'm a little bit older than him, but we hung just like whatever we do today. But we're not doing no illegal activities like back in the game.

You know how to make a redfish courtbouillon? I can try to tell you the best that I could. I'm not a guy who cooks per recipes, but you cook it with the head, everything on the fish, and after you cook him, you lift out the bones, get all the bones out. You cook it in a nice stew pan, with a lid, but when you're first cooking it, you're cooking it without the lid. You put tomatoes—real tomatoes, and you put it with olive oil, your little garlic, and some onions. You don't want to make it with no tomato paste. I'm giving you the old-school recipe. Today I would make it different. With my liver, I have to deal with food different.

My Aunt Gueneri would always take some chicken foots and throw that in [her courtbouillon]. After you put the top on, put some chicken foots in it, and then you add some more vegeterribles. Put in some carrots, and whatever you feel like putting in it—whatever you've got! That's usually what we call a hunter's stew, because you're hunting for whatever you've got in the kitchen. Put some celeries; it's always good to put the leaves of the celeries—not the most part of the celery, just them leaves and put in there. Cook it until it's real tender, then you've got something where you can eat all that meat from under the gills; there's some good flavor there. And a lot of people don't eat them, but I always like to eat the eyeballs too—you've just got to get the hard part out. The

little harder part in it, you don't want to eat that. Now, Wallace, he'd probably give you a whole other recipe, that's the difference. He'd cook a redfish courtbouillon totally different than I would. But that's Louisiana for you, south Louisiana.

I remember when I was a kid, my Aunt Gueneri used to always take acorns and cut them up and put that instead of pine nuts, because she was too cheeky to go buy pine nuts at the French Market or wherever they were selling them. She didn't want to waste no money, and she made everything from scratch. She made stock from scratch: duck stock, goose stock, any critter stock. And then she used that on a whole other dish. All the chefs from the restaurants went over to eat at her pad, because it was real close to all of them. She lived on Carrollton Avenue right off of Canal and Iberville. She used to make this dish called stuffed steak and it was just a little bitty piece of veal around a pie that had—it'd be like stuffed mirliton with shrimps in it, or stuffed butternut squash with some regular fish in it, and some eggplant with some crawfish meat in it, and no matter what way you cut, you was going to have something totally different in parts of it. I never had nothing like that. And them restaurant owners never got that. All them people used to come eat at my Aunt Gueneri's place, and she would cuss you out in a minute if you said, "Love your Italian cooking." She'd go off on him, say, "This is not *Italiano*, this is *Siciliano*!" That was a big thing because all of the people who came to New Orleans [from Italy] were Sicilian. They came here from Tunis, Africa, that little part of Tunisia. I remember the family on St. Philip Street across from a school. It looked like a religious church when you walked in the door to get your muffuletta sandwich. There were holy pictures

Dr. John at Voodoo

My Aunt Gueneri would put wild greens in a lot of food. There were dandelion greens, certain kinds of grass she put—not just any grass—and she picked them off the neutral ground. All of these things, she used them in her cooking. As a little kid, when I was a little weed-hopper, that was my job, to take my little wagon and put whatever. She'd go all the way to the French Market, say, she'd get a live chicken, and she would go all the way to another part of town, to some guy who had a Sicilian something. She would get that from him, and then we'd go all the way over by Broad, by the pumping station, and get something else, and then go all the way back to her pad, and I'd be worn out. She weren't even close to it. She put a clove of garlic in each shoe every day, and she was never sick.

My pa would take me, he taught me how to trap, how to fish, when I was a little bitty kid. We did all of that. Trap squirrels—you don't want to shoot a squirrel, because he's too little. So you want to trap him, you want to trap a coon—you want to trap every critter you can get your hands on. During the summer, you ate fish and a lot of different kinds of fish. And in the winter, you ate seasonably. This was before you had all of these stupid fast-food places all over the place.

Musicians all over south Louisiana used to call in when Johnny Jambalaya had a radio show, people would call in with a recipe. Now, nobody in my family had ever ate a choupique [a bowfin fish] but this guy figured out that if you cook them up really fast, and don't wait until you get home, then they're good to eat. We used to cut them up for crab bait, stuff like that. But with a soft-shell crab, it was a killer dish.

We like wild game, like the specklebelly goose. It's hard to get all of them things today because I don't want to

everywhere, up on the ceiling, all on the walls. They had a St. Joseph altar year round in that place, you felt like you were in some weird kind of church, and that was the place to get muffuletta sandwiches. It was my job, working in the studio band, with Cosimo [Matassa] to go get the muffuletta sandwiches for the gig. Stuff like that. Muffuletta sandwiches had a lot more on it than they say now. They had tons of kinds of meats and cheeses, plus they had chives and olive sauce and olive salad. They were so big, and everybody in the band would cut a piece off, cut them a slice, and everybody would be full. Everybody loved to eat that.

be popping no caps into nothing no more. It was a time, I didn't think half to shoot a duck or goose or whatever, but I've been shot too many times. Shot in this finger, in this cheek, in my butt. I've been shot through my knee, where my wife shot me, my first wife. She could shoot. She would have shot over me, but I panicked when I saw the piece—she'd already hit me with a skillet that day—and then she shanked me in my back, and when I woke up with a pillow over my face and her knees in my neck, I just threw her off. But when she walked in the room and I was knocked out loaded and she walked in there with a piece, I'm thinking, "She's going to shoot me." But she was going to shoot over me, just give me a warning. But I pushed the chair backwards and it went right in my knee. It was only because the chair went backwards and my knee was up.

My aunt would cook everything at her pad. She'd cook an eight-course meal in the course of every day. And you'd better be ready to eat just a little bit of this and a little bit of that because [otherwise] you weren't going to make it to the main course! Took me a long time to figure out how to get to the main course. That's what kids do anyway, eat everything that's in front of them. And that's what my family always told me, "You've got to eat, no matter what you put on your plate, you eat everything there." And that's a good way to eat. If you don't take it, you ain't got to eat it. No waste. There it is.

—Dr. John

*Wallace Boudreaux, on cooking with Dr. John:*

"We cook frog legs whenever we can get them. We've had them for breakfast. We've had them for dinner and lunch. Frog legs are a delicacy. People say, 'Don't it taste like chicken?' No, actually, it tastes like frog legs.

When I cook coon, 'What does it taste like?' Well, it tastes like coon. I usually put just a little Tony Chachere's, a little flour, and cayenne.

We get our meat from hunters. 'Hey, you want this? Hey, you want that? Would you like this? We've got enough—would you like some?' Sure!

I used to live in the woods when I was a little boy. Running away from foster homes and getting away, going hiding. Living in the woods. I'd just take off. Talking to people and learning how to trap and hunt, I used to survive in the woods. Catching raccoons, catching fish, catching rabbits and squirrels, making little traps. It was nice; I enjoyed myself, until I got poison ivy, and then I had to go to a hospital and the police came and arrested me, came to another welfare department. Cooking became essential. It became a necessity. Wild game is something I always enjoyed cooking because it's all there really was to eat.

I try to make sure Mac [Dr. John] gets to eat, but sometimes we bounce around from one session to the next, recordings and interviews, pictures or autographs. It's just non-stop. Mac loves food, but he's on a very specific diet. I cook a lot of greens for him, collard greens, turnip greens, and cabbage. I cook that for him, and he loves it.

We've known each other for a long, long time, since 1958. That's a while back, and we're still partners. Never had a hard word, never had an argument. And I love him like a brother. Do anything in the world for him, and he

Fried Frog Legs

it don't have none of that. Trapper Joe gives us things, alligator meat and turtle, we call it *cowan*, delicious, it's like a king's feast. And pheasant, too. But we don't eat a lot of things. We don't eat pork, no shellfish at all, because of the iodine. We have hepatitis C and the iodine affects that. So we're very conscientious about iodine.

We got these frog legs from friends out of Thibodaux. There are so many bullfrogs around there. Frogs are just blossoming."

## Fried Frog Legs

12 frog legs
2 cups milk
4 eggs
2 tablespoons Tony Chachere's Lite Creole Seasoning
Juice of ½ lemon
1 cup flour
1 teaspoon cayenne

knows it. The other day he said, 'You know what I love about you a lot? You're fiercely loyal.' Well, what are partners for? He just smiled.

I like keeping things simple, as simple as possible. Whatever it is I'm cooking, I never cook the same dish twice. Always adventuring, different methods of cooking—all good things are out there; they're available. If people would stop and think about what they're buying at the store, instead of just snatching things off the shelf without even knowing the ingredients. Golly! A lot of the words you can't even pronounce. There's a lot of preservatives and hormones. So wild game, honey, yes,

Soak frog legs in 1 cup of milk. Make egg wash by mixing the rest of the milk, eggs, Tony's, and lemon juice. Mix cayenne into flour in a separate bowl. Dip frog legs into flour mixture, then egg wash, then flour again. Fry in olive oil (about ½-inch deep) over medium heat, for 2-3 minutes on each side, until golden.

# The Gravy

## IN THE KITCHEN WITH

# Monk Boudreaux

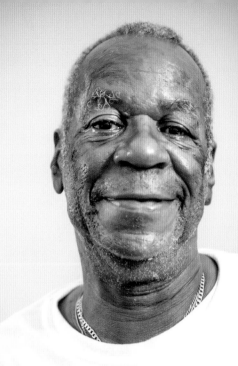

BIG CHIEF MONK BOUDREAUX CASTS A WIDE NET: "When I was a kid, I did never go outside. Always stayed inside, and my grandmother used to cook. I helped her cut up the seasoning. Then, when my grandmother died, I liked to stay home and watch my mom cook. I just wasn't interested in being outside. I don't go nowhere now, you know, unless I'm going fishing. You won't get any trouble, that's for one thing. Just stay inside, watching cooking shows on TV.

In the fall, I mostly cook greens—cabbage, mustard greens, turnip greens; rabbit, raccoon, venison in season. A lot of fish because I go fishing a lot. We go down to Port Sulphur and Empire. I have a small 14-foot flat, enough to get me around where I need to be. I design for the second lines, the fans and the stuff in there. Prince of Wales has 12 adults and six kids, that's what I'm working on now. So I can't go fishing until after this. I can't wait! When this is over with, that's where you're going to find me, sitting on some bayou.

I cook goat, the whole goat. Go get a goat up there in Boothville, up 90 going towards Houma. I soak him down in vinegar and a lot of seasonings—onion, garlic, bell pepper, celery—soak him down overnight. Put ice all over it, put the vinegar and the salt and the

"The alligator, the coon, and venison, all that's gone. Somebody eat it."

**BORN**
1941 in New Orleans, Louisiana

**NEIGHBORHOOD**
Central City

**INSTRUMENTS**
Vocals, tambourine, drums

**NOTABLE RECORDING**
"Footsteps," *Won't Bow Down*, 2011

**HOLY TRINITY**
Garlic, onion, bell pepper

pepper, maybe a little cayenne, and the next day he ready. Put him on the grill. Sometime, I run him in the oven first, at 300, kind of get him going, you know, and then go put him on the grill. You've got to cut the veins out, the silk running through it; same with the venison. They make the meat tough. After you get it nice and tender on the grill, you put the sauce on there, start rubbing it down with the sauce, slapping it on there. I buy regular barbecue sauce. I used to make one, but my daughter used to help me to make it so I don't make it no more. I just go buy me a sauce. I might add a little black pepper, a little honey, seasoning salt, lemon. Might put some oranges and squeeze in it. Put it on the ribs, come out real good. I might have goat, ribs, venison, coon, rabbit, squirrels. And there are hundreds of people out here, right out front my door. My mom used to do it when she was able; she used to feed everybody in the city.

For my roux, I just take a skillet, make it hot and pour the flour in there. That's to keep the grease down. I don't like all that grease. I don't even like butter. Got some in there that's been there a year or something. Doing the roux dry like this is easy, but if the phone rings, don't go answer, I'm telling you. You have to stand there and stir it. That's my cooking spoon over there, with the holes in it. I don't know why, but that's the one I like. I use it for everything.

Cooking is really easy, if you want to cook. I had to cook because I raised five kids by myself. I had to come home from work, cook for them, make sure they eat. And I knew how to cook. Now, I have seven grandchildren. The little girl, when I'm cleaning fish, she wants a knife, she wants to clean some fish, so I give her a butter knife, 'Try this.' I've got a lot of knives and they're sharp. I love knives. I've got a lot more in the drawer right here. I buy knives for me

everywhere. I do a lot of cleaning, a lot of different wildlife and fish, and you've got to have a good knife, so I keep a lot of knives. All kind; I love knives. My friends say, 'Why do you buy so many fishing poles?' and I say, 'They all do something different, that's why.' Same thing with knives.

Today, I'm making some filé gumbo with shrimp, crab, sausage, chicken, and chicken gizzards—a lot of work for people who don't like to cook. Like making an Indian suit, that's a lot of work too. But, hey, not for the Indians. It's easy, just take a little while.

A friend of mine, he goes up to the country and gets coons from the trappers. I always get five or six, because the people who follow me on Mardi Gras Day, they love it. The most important thing in cooking a raccoon is you have to musk him, you have to get the musks out. A large coon got 32 musks, and most of them come out when they pull the hide off, but you've got to make sure you get them all out. When I do that, I put my glasses on. The meat is like a dark red, and the musks are a little lighter than that so you can see them. You just got to know what you're looking for. After you musk him, wash him down real good, put him in a big pot and parboil him, because he's real tough. Take a little seasoning salt, cayenne pepper, black pepper. Sometime I put liquid crab boil in there. Parboil him until you can flip the meat; breaks right loose. I do them whole because I like to barbecue the whole thing. Once you do that, you got him. Some people don't wait until you put the barbecue sauce on there. They're going to eat it and love it. You know, I get a lot of this: 'I don't eat this, I don't eat that,' but when I go out there, the alligator, the coon, and venison, all that's gone. Somebody eat it.

Raccoon, that's Mardi Gras evening. I generally get them for Christmas, but I hold them until Mardi Gras because I know they'll get eaten up then. Then a friend of mine, he always comes from Detroit. I taught him how to musk them, so I don't have to do that. I just continue sewing. He call me, 'Come check it out!' And I come check it out, put my glasses on. They're like a football shape. I learned that when I was about 12-13 years old, how to musk them. One time I was selling papers, and I see this sign way down on Rampart Street say 'Coons.' I said to myself I was going to buy one for mommy, and the guy in there asked me if I knew how to musk them and I said 'No.' He said, 'Let me show you.' Some of them are as big as a little fingernail. Once you take them out you can't beat the taste. Coon, that was one of the first foods, you know, back in the day. Pioneers and all that. They had raccoon hats. What do you think they did with the meat? Threw it away?"

Monk Boudreaux at Hogs for the Cause
Photo by Golden G. Richard, III

# Baby Alligator Gravy

"Cayenne is good for wildlife, all of it. It adds another notch to it, but my old lady can't eat nothing spicy, so, mess my day up."

2 pounds baby alligator legs, skinned
   (look like chicken drumettes)
2 tablespoons margarine
1 small onion, diced
4 green onions, chopped
¼ bunch parsley, chopped
½ bell pepper, diced
½ jar Ragu Old World Style Traditional Pasta Sauce
1 teaspoon garlic powder
4 tablespoons dry roux
1 cup water
Salt and black pepper to taste
Cayenne to taste

Brown alligator in margarine in a large skillet. Set meat aside. Add onion, green onions, parsley, and bell pepper to skillet and sauté until soft. Add Ragu, garlic powder, and roux. Thin with water. Simmer for 30 minutes. Season to taste with salt, black pepper, and cayenne. Add alligator back in and simmer, covered, for another 30 minutes.

IN THE KITCHEN WITH

# Johnny Vidacovich

"The whole trick to making this dish work out is to have a wife."

**JOHNNY VIDACOVICH ISN'T AFRAID TO DIE, UNLESS HE RUNS OUT OF SPAGHETTI:** "The poem, yes. We call it 'Getting Ready Spaghetti.' The name of the poem is 'Oh, it's Fun to Play the Drums,' but the best part of playing the drums is eating spaghetti.

*Oh, it's fun to play the drums.*
*Getting ready, eating spaghetti.*
*Going to the gig, feeling like a pig.*
*Oh, it's fun to play the drums.*
*Stomach's full of music's fuel*
*that makes the bouncing balls of*
*sound and time go touching all*
*over your skin.*
*Oh, it's fun to play the drums.*
*Eating spaghetti, getting ready.*
*Going to the gig, feeling like a pig.*

Now, the protein in here is great. By the time you get to work it's like [snaps fingers]. Protein going to work, you know. Pasta get you through the gig. I try to eat a lot of pasta. I was raised by my Sicilian

**BORN**
1949 in New Orleans, Louisiana

**NEIGHBORHOOD**
Mid-City

**INSTRUMENTS**
Drums, vocals

**NOTABLE RECORDING**
"Long Song," *My Backyard*,
Mose Allison, 1989

**HOLY TRINITY**
Olive oil, garlic, basil

Previous page: Johnny Vidacovich's wife Deborah oversees the cooking process.

grandparents all my life, so I had pasta about four times a week, in different forms and variations. The whole trick to making this dish work out is to have a wife. Ha! No, the secret to this dish is good cheese. Spend money on cheese, spend the money on cheese.

If you say, 'Johnny, we're having pasta at my house to-night,' I'm not going to ask 'What kind?'—I'm not going to say that because I know I'm going to like it. If it's some-thing I've never had before, then I'll eat slow. Pasta can hold anything together. I wouldn't put a can of tuna fish in it, though.

Italian is my first choice. When I'm out with Astral Proj-ect, we eat healthy. Tony [Dagradi]'s a vegetarian, so he's a problem. You've got to make sure the food is up to his standards, with no animals in it. Tony will eat no bullshit. No eggs. No butter. Bless his heart and their hearts, be-cause James [Singleton] is a real bitch when it comes to—can I edit some words out?—he's very conscious about food. They're googled up, 'Seven miles, take a right' and you walk into Happy Chopstick and there's a Mexican back there. I don't say nothing. I say, 'Okay, brother. Just give me a pair of chopsticks and a tamale.'

My mother-in-law cooks fat-boy meals. She loves me because I go over there with a fork in each hand. You're watching the right guy because I love to eat and I'm skinny as a rail. That's all right, I'm healthy.

My grandmother cooked hamburgers on Saturdays. That was traditional, every Saturday. But they were not like anybody else's hamburgers. Most people take hamburger meat, make a patty, fry it. My grandmother cut up a little onion, a little green bell pepper. She took an egg, she took a little Italian breadcrumbs—could have been celery in there, maybe garlic, but she'd only put a

little because we were young and garlic was strong to us. Now, I can sit down with an apple, piece of cheese and eat a whole bulb of garlic. Raw!

I like coffee, and I like it all kinds of different ways. After Katrina, I got the Maserati of coffee makers. My grandmother used to give us coffee when we were little kids, before we'd go to bed. Love coffee, my whole life, but not that hotel coffee. That shit will give you the shakes.

I have low blood sugar. Have to watch it. I've never passed out on stage, but there's been times when I was out, passed out, and people freaking out that I've had a heart attack. Man, two things; I need an apple and I need a Coca-Cola. Cola get me right up; apple keep me going. Want me up right now? Give me a Coke real quick; back it up with an apple.

My grandmother's red gravy was good. She made a great meatball sandwich: French bread, mash a meatball down on that, put some red gravy on it. I know that as long as I eat spaghetti, I won't be afraid. It's going to be great to die, it's going to be great!"

## Getting Ready Spaghetti

1 head roasted garlic
¼ cup pine nuts
¼ cup olive oil
¼ cup basil chiffonade
1 handful cherry tomatoes, cut in half
1 pound pasta, cooked al dente
¼ cup grated parmesan cheese

Roast garlic at 300 degrees for 30 minutes: Cut the top off the head, exposing the cloves, and rub a few drops of olive

Getting Ready Penne

Johnny Vidacovich with Ike Stubblefield at the Blue Nile.
"Is it time for cookies and milk? I'll share.
You can have the bigger half."

oil on top and over the skin. Garlic is ready when cloves are soft enough that you can squeeze them out.

Toast pine nuts in a dry skillet until golden, stirring/shaking constantly. Heat oil in a large skillet. Add roasted garlic cloves, pine nuts, basil chiffonade (stack leaves, roll into a fat roll and cut to make long, thin strips), and tomatoes and cook until warm, about a minute. Toss with pasta in a large serving bowl and serve immediately, covered with parmesan cheese.

## IN THE KITCHEN WITH

# Ingrid Lucia

**INGRID LUCIA'S LEMON GARLIC PASTA MAKES YOU FEEL BETTER IMMEDIATELY:** "I'm not the best cook in the family. My husband Dwight is. The dishes that I do know how to make were kind of out of necessity from all of our years in Mexico, so I'm more of a Mexican dish maker. But I love making pasta, too. It's a neutral. With pasta, you can pretty much put anything in it and give it different flavors and variety, so I like to mess around. Just take what we have in the house and make new recipe ideas, which sometimes can be great and sometimes can be horrible. It's a big adventure every time, but the family is pretty open-minded to at least try a couple of bites.

When Dwight and I first got together, I made him an authentic Mexican tortilla soup, which had boiled eggs in it. It's pretty hearty and hardcore, with homemade tortillas. He took that idea and improved on it and now he makes this incredible tortilla soup with chips. It's an award-winning soup.

We spent pretty much every winter from the time I was nine until I was 18 traveling around Mexico playing music with our family band. One of the times that we went down there, we ended up taking a chef and her family on the road with us. They were from this

**BORN**
1970 in San Francisco, California

**NEIGHBORHOOD**
Mid-City

**INSTRUMENTS**
Vocals, drums, bass

**NOTABLE RECORDING**
"Funny Boy," *Midnight Rendezvous*, 2010

**HOLY TRINITY**
Lime, garlic, cilantro

Mexican circus, and she taught us a lot of her recipes and dishes—anything from scrambling eggs with green beans to her tortilla soup. She made these potato burritos that were amazing. She took very simple foods and only had two burners, and she would make a huge pot of soup for the whole circus. It would have nopales, which is cactus—you can peel it, it's really yummy. Basically, she took staples and very little meat or fish to flavor them, but it wasn't a high protein thing and it didn't cost a lot of money. When we were being musicians and not doing so great, I would remember all those recipes and try to mess around with her ideas and make dinner for everyone.

We had to cook growing up because we were very, very poor. Our staples were beans, rice, eggs. Part of the survival thing was, at a young age—from like 10 on up to our teenage years—we had to all take turns making dishes. But there were no rules or boundaries put on us, so we were exploring and experimenting. Brown rice was our staple. That was supposed to be the healthiest thing we could eat, so every meal had to have a brown rice base and we could add any kind of fruit, vegetable, or protein that we wanted to. Grated carrots with peanuts and raisins, all kinds of combinations, until we found some that worked and were really good. And we're all healthy. Nobody got sick, so it worked. Some of the dishes weren't so great, but we stayed healthy.

New Orleans is pretty similar to Mexico, I think, in that there are many poor people who make poor man's dishes. A lot of our foods are based around beans and rice. We like spicy food; both cultures are very spice-oriented. And it's a very communal, family-oriented culture. Families get together on certain days of the week and do their cooking and their grilling. People love barbequed meats—

that's similar as well. Really, there's a lot of Latin influence in New Orleans culture, so it's kind of strange that it's having a comeback now with all the Latinos coming to work on the houses. People are bouncing off each other again. People might be able to connect with their roots some more. We'll see.

I'm really trying to open my mind, going into the grocery store and looking around for new items to experiment with. Instead of bringing home an apple, I'll bring home a pear or a mango and try to use that. Having a seven-year-old makes it tough because she doesn't even like mashed potatoes. I try to keep the food simple for Ava, but then I mess around and make Dwight miserable."

## Lemon Garlic Pasta

"It's a good winter dish because when you're coming down with a cold, all the garlic just knocks it out right away. It makes you feel better immediately. Make it for your honey!"

1 box rigatoni pasta
2 tablespoons pine nuts
2 lemons
6 or more garlic cloves
1 cup freshly grated parmesan cheese
½ cup olive oil

Boil pasta according to directions on box. Toast pine nuts in a dry frying pan over low to medium heat, stirring constantly. Finely grate zest of 1 lemon into a large bowl. Add juice from 1½ lemons. Press garlic cloves and add

Lemon Garlic Rigatoni

Ingrid Lucia at Three Muses, with Simon Lott on drums

to zest/juice, as well as parmesan and olive oil. Stir as to make an emulsion. When pasta is al dente, drain and mix with lemon garlic dressing. Serve hot, with toasted pine nuts on top.

## IN THE KITCHEN WITH

# Antoinette K-Doe

**BORN**
1943 in New Orleans, Louisiana

**NEIGHBORHOOD**
Tremé

**INSTRUMENTS**
Vocals

**NOTABLE RECORDING**
Appeared with Ernie K-Doe in the movie *Happy Here and Now* (2002)

**HOLY TRINITY**
Garlic, garlic, garlic

**WHEN SHE MADE GROCERIES, ANTOINETTE K-DOE WALKED DOWN ALL THE AISLES BUT TWO:** "I just love to cook. When I'm cooking, my mother and grandmother are inside of me, so that means a lot. And that's all I know, is to cook and feed people. My grandmother was a seamstress and a darn good cook. As a kid, I didn't go outside to play with the children. I always wanted to learn, learn how to cook, and learn how to sew. And my grandmother taught me that. I am a seamstress and a designer, newspaper patterns, or out of my head.

My grandmother and my mother raised me. My father was absent and you know how that goes, right? I grew up in Gert Town and then we moved to the Ninth Ward.

The cooking and eating we had back then, I would describe it today as a work of art. It was something that people took pride in. They didn't go to restaurants. We were too poor. So my grandmother would cook; and we had one neighbor, she farmed chickens. She had a lot of eggs, so my grandmother and her would swap. Eggs for whatever we grew and whatever anybody else grew. We grew snap beans, somebody else grew greens, and they swapped.

We went to the market and bought some things—like if our squash didn't do good, or mirlitons or something, then we went to buy it. But everybody had mirlitons. They grew on your fence, made it look pretty. Whatever neighbor would have pecan trees, we'd go pick pecans. That's how we made it; you learned how to survive.

I plant peppers, hot peppers, shallots, and mustard greens— enough mustard greens to give to all our senior-citizen neighbors. I do have flowers in there, but I have to find myself another little spot to plant mustard greens, because I love mustards. Flowers and vegetables, I like both of them, but I know what I need. I need a lot of veggies. Flowers are beautiful, they bring you joy, but they don't take care of your body.

I don't cook just for myself or four people. My grandmother always said, 'If you have six people in your family, you make sure you cook for 12.' Because somebody always comes into your house, and then you can offer them something to eat. But if you cook the amount for your family, you cannot share with anybody else. And that's what I do; I share. So when I make cornbread, I make a sheet pan of cornbread.

My grandmother had some very, very old recipes. I have two of them that I cook all the time myself. Red beans and gumbo. And I can tell you this: I don't do a gumbo with a roux. The recipe is a very, very secret recipe. I have been asked to go on TV and cook it, but I don't want to give up my recipe—it's my grandmother's recipe. The only person that knows that recipe is me and Ernie K-Doe. Now if he'll tell you, you're okay.

Ernie's favorite meal was red beans and rice. We used to go out for dinner and come home and he would say, 'Baby, I want some red beans.'

In the supermarket, there are only two aisles I don't go down. That's the baby food and the dog food. I don't have no more babies, and I sure don't have time for no dogs."

*Ben Sandmel on Antoinette K-Doe:*

"Antoinette K-Doe was both a great cook and a woman with strong nurturing instincts who offered free food to everyone who walked into the Mother-In-Law Lounge. There was always a crock pot or two behind the bar. The two dishes I remember Antoinette cooking most often were red beans and rice and a thick, hearty vegetable beef 'soup,' as she called it, although its consistency was more like that of a stew. Both were delicious, and offered graciously, with a touch of maternal insistence. Like most mothers, Antoinette might take a bit of offense at anyone who passed on her hospitality, with the implied message that they just weren't getting enough nutrition.

In the days after Katrina, even though Antoinette had no water or electricity, she still managed to cook vast amounts of food—almost on an institutional scale—and offer it at no charge to cops, National Guard members, relief workers, reporters, and traumatized New Orleanians left homeless by the storm. Ernie K-Doe had come to her in a vision, she explained, and told her to 'feed the people.' This she did, at her own expense, asking nothing in return, until she passed away on Mardi Gras Day in 2009."

*Ben Sandmel is a New Orleans-based journalist, folklorist, and drummer. He is the author of* Zydeco!, *a collaborative book with photographer and musician Rick Olivier (also in this book), published by the University Press of Mississippi in 1999, and* Ernie K-Doe: The R&B Emperor of New Orleans, *published by the Historic New Orleans Collection in 2012.*

Cornbread in a skillet on the stovetop is easy to burn, but cast-iron skillets can go in the oven too

Antoinette K-Doe and the mannequin resembling her deceased husband Ernie K-Doe in St. Louis Cemetery No. 2
Photo by Erika Goldring, All Saints Day, 2007

# K-Doe Cornbread

¼ cup olive oil
2 cups yellow cornmeal
2 cups flour
1 tablespoon baking powder
1 teaspoon salt
¼ cup sugar
2 cups milk
4 eggs, lightly beaten
1 stick butter, softened

Pour olive oil into a 13" x 9" baking pan and place it in an oven pre-heated to somewhere between 350 and 400 degrees (you know your oven). Stir all the dry ingredients together in a bowl. Add milk and eggs, and stir until everything comes together. Pour batter into hot oil (creating a crispy bottom crust), and bake for 20-30 minutes, until golden. Spread butter on top and bake for another 5-10 minutes.

**IN THE KITCHEN WITH**

# Brint Anderson

"I go to restaurant supply places just like I go to music stores."

**BORN**
1954 in Natchez, Mississippi

**NEIGHBORHOOD**
Indigo Estates, Laplace

**INSTRUMENTS**
Guitar, vocals, bass

**NOTABLE RECORDING**
"I Knew This Would Happen," *I Knew This Would Happen*, 1997

**HOLY TRINITY**
Butter, onion, poblano pepper

**BRINT ANDERSON GIVES HIS FOOD THAT LAPLACE TOUCH:**
"I was born in Natchez. We always ate well because my mother was a great cook. She was one of the first housewives in Natchez to have Julia Child's *Mastering the Art of French Cooking*. In fact, I've got it here. I got all her books after she passed away in '04. Her name was Katherine, but everybody called her Kitty. Here, I wanted to show you. I saved this old clipping. My mother won a new pair of high heels from Burns shoe store on Main Street in Natchez with her chicken recipe. It was a housewife competition, and this was the '60s. Maybe she adapted duck à l'orange and just added the bacon. As far as I know she invented it. She used to make it around the holidays and it made the house smell great. This was the first time she entered a competition. I was 12.

My mother was a strong, determined person. She'd bring us to New Orleans and take us to Antoine's and teach us culture. We grew up learning all the ballroom dances. After we'd gone off to college, she started her own travel agency. This was back when travel agents could do pretty well because you didn't have computers. She traveled the world.

I make her chicken a couple of times a year, but I cook a variety of things. I love French cooking. To me, if you want to be a good cook, you have to learn some French technique. When I first went to culinary school at Delgado, *Mastering the Art of French Cooking* was my bible. It really breaks down the basics of stocks and sauces. I made this [turning pages], Lobster Thermidor, on Christmas eve. Only a French chef could come up with this, because it's nothing but butter and cream and reduction sauces involving the fat in the head of the lobsters.

I have an outdoor kitchen. We used to have a small patio and when we put the swimming pool in, I saved the lumber and built the cooking shed out back. I'm really getting into charcuterie. I want to get better at making pâtés. I want to master pâté *en croute*, just one time. Just to say I could do it. I've smoked meats for years and I've made galantines and boulettes, which are almost like a mousseline. Galantine is where you debone a bird and take the meat and make a stuffing and keep the skin intact, pull it back together, wrap it with bacon and toothpicks, and bake it.

I already had a cast-iron smoker that handles 50-60 pounds of meat, and I've always cooked barbecue. Then my brother-in-law gave me a stainless steel propane grill, and I have a crawfish boiling pot that can cook a whole sack at a time. The place where I get my fresh chickens, in Reserve, has all these great outdoor cooking accessories, so that's where I got the two-top burner. It's pretty much a complete outdoor kitchen, with all I need. I like to collect my tools. Ever since I got into this, I go to restaurant-supply places just like I go to music stores. These are my mother's poultry scissors that she bought in Italy.

I've tried not to mess with this recipe too much. It's basically the same as my mom's, except for the zest, and the Worchestershire, and the hot sauce, and the horseradish. I can't help it; it's my New Orleans influence. My mom's recipe says bacon, but I use andouille to give it that Laplace touch."

A CHICKEN RECIPE brought Mrs. William Korber of Vidalia a pair of high-fashion Life Stride dress shoes for fall from Burns Shoe Store in Natchez. Andrew Burns fits the shoe on Mrs. Koerber's foot. Mrs. Koerber's recipe was for Curry Glazed Chicken.

## Mother Kitty's Curry Glazed Chicken

1 (10½-ounce) can beef consommé
2½ tablespoons flour
¼ cup orange marmalade
1 onion, finely diced
6 ounces andouille, finely diced
1 tablespoon curry powder
2 tablespoons Heinz chili sauce
2 tablespoons lemon juice
1 teaspoon prepared horseradish
1 teaspoon hot sauce
1 teaspoon Worchestershire sauce
1 teaspoon orange and/or lemon zest

Brint Anderson shows off Mother Kitty's Curry Glazed Chicken and the cooking shed he built in his backyard

Brint Anderson at Margaritaville in the French Quarter

2 chickens, quartered, brushed with butter and seasoned with salt and pepper

Whisk together consommé and flour. Add remaining ingredients, except for chicken. Simmer to thicken, about 5 minutes. Set aside. Bake chicken at 400 degrees for 20 minutes. Remove juices. Spoon half of the curry glaze over chicken and bake for 20 minutes. Spoon remaining glaze over chicken and bake for another 20 minutes.

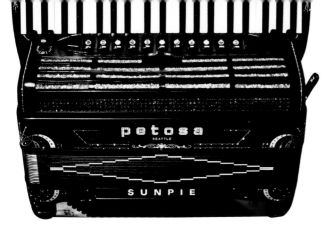

**IN THE KITCHEN WITH**

# Sunpie Barnes

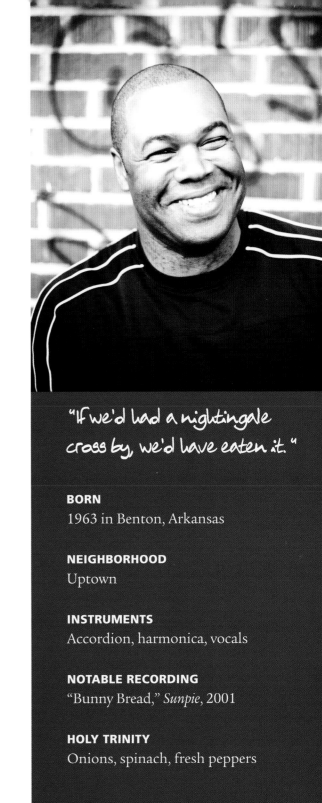

"If we'd had a nightingale cross by, we'd have eaten it."

**BORN**
1963 in Benton, Arkansas

**NEIGHBORHOOD**
Uptown

**INSTRUMENTS**
Accordion, harmonica, vocals

**NOTABLE RECORDING**
"Bunny Bread," *Sunpie*, 2001

**HOLY TRINITY**
Onions, spinach, fresh peppers

**SUNPIE BARNES HAS COOKED AND EATEN EVERY SONG-BIRD IN THE BOOK:** "I don't cook every day. All the different types of work that I do: I have my regular nine-to-five working for the National Park Service, have been doing that forever, and I'm a working musician, and I do other things also, so I'm on the run a lot. But I like to cook because I like to eat. It's not every day, though. Can't tell that lie! But I live with a gourmet cook, so I don't cry about it.

I was raised up in the Deep South so I can cook all kinds of soul food, southern cuisine, but also stuff that's here in Louisiana. I started to cook alligator sauce piquante today but ended up not doing it because I've eaten so many tomatoes lately. So I'm cooking salmon and white shrimp—white shrimp are beautiful right now. I love fish; I've been eating fish a lot lately because I've been fishing also. I didn't catch salmon, of course, but I've been going out in the swamps, getting some bass and stuff like that.

As a child, we dug everything out of the woods that could be dug out and eaten. Did a lot of hunting and fishing; I guess what people call subsistence living. We were raised with a huge garden, some people talk about a vegetable garden, but ours was about two-

and-a-half acres. Peas, corn, all varieties of collard greens, mustard greens, turnip greens, rutabaga, black-eyed peas, green beans, snap beans, blue runners, crowders, tomatoes, okra, squash, cabbage, watermelon, cantaloupe. No carrots and broccoli! This is the South, and carrots and broccoli are not soul food. Squash is soul food. Pumpkin—same family—not soul food. [laughs] We grew some spinach, but it was mainly greens. It was our yard and our neighbor's yard, so we shared fields. My parents were sharecroppers. We shared a couple of fields. I grew up on the edge of Benton, Arkansas, in a community called Gravel Hill, right on the edge of the Mississippi Delta. I came from Blues Country but the accordion really struck a chord with me.

I used to be allergic to shrimp, made me deathly ill. The first time it hit me so hard it put me down on the ground. Thought I was going to die. Cramps, and I couldn't breathe. I'm allergic to the iodine. King crabs and stuff like that put the hurt on me. Hurt my feelings too. I had these friends when I was working at Jean Lafitte and they loved me and they had this restaurant. All they served was gumbo and po-boys, basically all shrimp. They served this big ol' bowl of gumbo that was nothing but shrimp and I couldn't get it across. 'Huh?' So I was sitting there. 'You want some more gumbo?' Finally, I had to say, 'Look, I have to tell you, I think I'm allergic to shrimp.' They said, 'Huh?' 'Huh?' He said, 'Mama, come here!' She came out the kitchen. 'What is it?' He said, 'Mama, he's allergic to shrimps!' She said, 'Huh? Oh, oh,' and she sat down as if somebody had died. 'Oh, no... You're allergic to shrimp, how could that happen to you?' And she looked at me and she said, 'Boo, what are you going to eat?!'

I've fished and cleaned fish my whole life. There's not much to think about, you just do it. Cleaning and filleting fish, yeah. Cleaning wild game, yeah. Deer, hogs, rabbit, squirrel, raccoon, we ate it all. Birds. I think I've eaten every songbird known to mankind. You name it. Name one! If we'd had a nightingale cross by, we'd have eaten it. But my favorite bird, actually, is robin. Still. But as we grew older, we learned that these were songbirds. We were like, 'What?! Songbirds?' In the countryside, boys all bird-hunt. So we're out bird-hunting and this man stopped us, he said, 'Come over here, boys. You know, it's against the law to hunt songbirds. Let me see what you've got.' So we were like, 'Songbirds? These ain't songbirds.' We had a bunch of robins. 'Robins don't sing. Mockingbirds sing.' And the man cracked up laughing, 'No, these are all songbirds.' So we had to go home and take out some books and look this stuff up. 'Craziest crap I ever heard of.'

Robin is excellent. You need a bunch of them because it's not the biggest bird in the world. Maybe 15 to a pan. We'd bake them in the oven and they were great. Just salt and pepper and Worchestershire sauce. Snap some lemons around that sucker and turn 'em loose in the oven.

In college, the first ornithology class I was in, my professor came to me and said, 'You're doing a good job. I've never seen a freshman that knew this many birds before. How did you learn so much about birds?' I looked at him and I said, 'I've eaten every bird in this class.'"

Blackened Shrimp, Latin style

Sunpie Barnes at Bayou Boogaloo
Photo by Golden G. Richard, III

# Blackened Shrimp

Showering shrimp in lime juice somehow helps Sunpie Barnes overcome his allergy to the crustaceans.

1 tablespoon olive oil
12 large fresh shrimp, heads removed
Sea salt
1 lime, cut in half

Pour oil into a hot frying pan; add shrimp and sprinkle with sea salt. Cook over high heat for a minute; squeezing half the lime over shrimp. When shells begin to blacken on the bottom, turn shrimp over, squeezing the other lime half over shrimp. Cook until shrimp are pink. Serve immediately.

## IN THE KITCHEN WITH

# Greg Schatz

*"You can get into trouble hurrying in the kitchen."*

**FOR GREG SCHATZ, THE SECRET TO COOKING IS NOT GETTING TOO HYPER:** "I worked at restaurants coming up, several of them. I worked at a few vegetarian restaurants in Ithaca, New York, my hometown, and I worked at a deli run by Hungarian Jews that had a really good chicken soup with matzo balls. I was mainly the carrot cutter.

I've been working towards getting more into the garden, and it makes choices a little easier. What am I going to put on that pizza? I think pesto! We have so much basil and eggplant, so it's going to be pesto and eggplant.

Around the time I moved to New Orleans in 1995, I started doing cabbage rolls, stuffed cabbage rolls. I make them Eastern-European style, a rice filling with beef, sautéed onions and peppers, or whatever you want in there. I do it once or twice a year. The last time I did it, my neighbor brought kielbasa and we chopped that up.

Last year, we got into using the pizza stone a lot. I found this Indian recipe for a tomato sauce that had coconut milk in it, and all the spices are bloomed beforehand. I put a lot of cumin, and then you finish it off with fresh cilantro. That's a good sauce. Bloomed means you put the spices in the hot oil in the beginning when you

**BORN**
1970 in Ithaca, New York

**NEIGHBORHOOD**
Bywater

**INSTRUMENTS**
Piano, vocals, accordion, bass

**NOTABLE RECORDING**
"Don't Give Up on Love,"
*Where the River Meets the Railroad Tracks,*
2012

**HOLY TRINITY**
Onion, garlic, beans

start cooking, let it develop its bouquet, before you put your other ingredients in there.

I think I should stop messing with this dough right now. I'm being too overactive. I'm being a bit cautious, and I'm leaving the grill on low. I'm afraid of it burning. Time actually goes by a lot quicker than you think.

Pizza is one of these things where we've had parties. But what is much more of a staple for me is black beans. I like to make a big pot of beans. It's just something I do very regularly, with a lot of cumin. I make beans a couple of times a month, a big pot that will last several days.

Lime, or local oranges, satsumas, I love to use citrus with beans. Make a reduction with the juice and put a little bit of pulp in there too. It's great. I'm into flexible things where you can adjust, depending on what the variables are, sort of controlling the thing. Starting a lot of things by sweating the onions and putting garlic in it, and that, for me, can go in so many different directions.

In the summer, I like cooking salad a lot. I know that doesn't make sense, cooking salad, but we eat a lot of salads. Sautéing tofu and putting it on top of a salad, making a marinade for the tofu, a ginger-tamari-rice-wine-vinegar sauce, or salad dressing, and sometimes having it in a rice bowl, depending on what you're in the mood for, with sautéed greens and other vegetables, maybe with a thin peanut sauce, cooking it down with spices and hot chili peppers. Use that on top of the bowl and maybe some pumpkin seeds. Basically a rice and vegetable bowl, like a cooked salad. Or use similar ingredients and put them on a fresh bed of greens. Salad is hard to come by in the summer, really hard to grow. If I could grow salad in the summertime, I would.

Pizza on the grill is a different animal, not what you'd get in a store. I've tried to come up with a crust that has structural integrity. When you hold it, it doesn't droop all the way down. I am not sure I accomplished it this time, but you should be able to hold your little slice of pizza. These ones will be fine, actually. If you cut them into quarters they are so small they won't droop. Right angles right there. Once I did them in halves and it worked pretty good, but I want structural integrity.

Sometimes, where I trip up with cooking is sometimes I get in too big of a hurry. You can get into trouble hurrying in the kitchen."

# Grilled Mini-Pizza St. Claude

**Rustic pizza dough**

1½ cups flour
1 cup whole wheat flour
½ cup cornmeal
1 envelope yeast (about 2 teaspoons)
2 teaspoons coarse salt
1 tablespoon fresh rosemary
3 tablespoons extra virgin olive oil

Combine dry ingredients and rosemary in a bowl. Add 1 cup warm water and olive oil, then add more water slowly until you have a firm but workable dough. Make four balls. Place balls in a container with a cloth on top and let rise for one hour. Roll out dough (in cornmeal) into circles about 6 inches in diameter and a quarter-inch thick.

Grill pizzas by placing dough disks directly on grate. Bake until disks can be flipped easily with a spatula (4-5 minutes). At the same time, grill thin slices of small

Grilled Mini-Pizza St. Claude

Greg Schatz at Three Muses, joined by Rosalie Ashton-Washington, a.k.a. Lady Tambourine of New Orleans

eggplant drizzled with olive oil in a pan, until tender. Flip dough disks and cover with a thin layer of either fresh tomato sauce or pesto. Sprinkle feta cheese or garlic chèvre cheese (from Royals Goat Dairy at the Crescent City Farmer's Market) on top. Remove pizzas when bottoms are lightly browned and toppings are hot (about 5 minutes). Add eggplant and some chopped fresh basil. Drizzle with olive oil and sprinkle with red pepper flakes. Cut into quarters and eat with washed hands.

**Fresh tomato sauce**

Sweat 2 diced onions in 2 tablespoons olive oil; add 3 cloves of garlic (minced) and 5-6 diced tomatoes. Simmer down until thick. Add salt and pepper to taste.

**Quick pesto**

Run 1 cup fresh basil in a food processor with just enough olive oil to help it chop up nice and smooth. Add ½ cup walnuts and 3 cloves garlic, and chop until fine. Add salt to taste.

**IN THE KITCHEN WITH**

# Miss Sophie Lee

**BORN**
1969 in Joliet, Illinois

**NEIGHBORHOOD**
Marigny

**INSTRUMENTS**
Vocals, piano, guitar

**NOTABLE RECORDING**
"Tallulah Moon," *Tallulah Moon*, 2010

**HOLY TRINITY**
Soy sauce, sesame oil, garlic

**THE DUMPLING SHAPE MATTERS FOR MISS SOPHIE LEE:**
"Korean food is a lot of little dishes, basically tapas, but they call it *banchan*. You have your bowl of rice and then all around you have all the little side dishes, one of which is always kimchi. And you're picking, you share, it's communal. Another dish is bean sprouts, which is called *kohng namool*. Basically it's mung bean sprouts, or green bean sprouts. Also spinach, which is called *shigumchi namool*. I did not make kimchi today because it takes a little longer. I buy it from the oriental market on Transcontinental in Metairie, right off Veterans, a wonderful Korean grocery store. Hong Kong Market [on the West Bank] is wonderful too, but it's pan-Asian. The store on Transcontinental is the only exclusively Korean grocery store. They used to have two. There was one over on Severn, but post-Katrina that's gone. Korean food is spicy. And the fermentation, a lot of people don't like, but I love it.

Today I'm making—we grew up calling them egg rolls, but they're essentially gyosa—it's a wonton wrap with a meat filling, and the Korean word for that is *mandu*. But growing up, my mother always just called them egg rolls. We'd all sit around the kitchen table helping her fill them. In Korean stores, you'll find square wrappers. This week they were out, they only had them in rounds. But I cut them—don't tell anybody. A Korean egg roll is going to be a triangle, rather than the crescent shape, which is more Japanese or Chinese. Traditionally, the filling is either ground pork or ground beef, or a combination. My mother always used beef.

I don't make this with my daughters yet, but I imagine I will when they're older. For kids, this is endless fun. For adults, it might be perhaps a little monotonous. But I remember being a child and having hours of fun filling these. It was a community project, a family project. It never seemed like cooking was work. It was me and my mom and my sisters—they're a little bit older—and my mom's best friend, and she had a daughter my age so we grew up together.

My mom and her girlfriend would always get together, every weekend. They'd cook, and then we'd sit around and watch them cook, help them cook. I remember very distinctly sometimes not wanting to be there, because you're young and you want to run around, and I remember her telling me—she was very emphatic: 'I want you to watch what I'm doing. I want you to learn these recipes, because you can take this with you forever, and then you will teach your daughters.' I didn't know the value of that then. Young, you don't know, but now that I'm older and I have my own children and she's passed away, it resonates. I always will remember that; I'll always be grateful to her for making me stand there and watch because you keep a part of the ones you love through cooking and by passing this down to your own children. I regretted her not teaching me the language, but I will forever be grateful for her teaching me the cooking because that way I feel close to her.

My mom passed away in '04 here in New Orleans. She came down to live with me in '01. We lived on Royal. I'm really happy that she had a chance to experience New Orleans before she passed away, because now this is my home. And I'm not going anywhere, and now it's my daughters' home.

I try to do a Korean dinner where we invite friends over a few times a year, especially around the holidays, whenever there is family in town. And John [Rodli, her husband], before my mom passed away, he got to know her and she actually started teaching him how to cook Korean. After I'd go to bed, they'd stay up and cook. She taught him how to make kimchi soup, *kimchi jjigae*. He's become quite the Korean chef.

I never met my Korean grandmother. She never made it over to the States. She passed away when I was 10. But when I was born, she told my mother that I would be a singer, without ever having met me.

After I moved here I found out that my father's mother was from Tallulah, Louisiana. Something was drawing me here. The last 10 years of my life, I've connected the dots and everything has tied together around the women in my life."

# Korean Egg Rolls

Koreans don't distinguish between breakfast, lunch, or dinner, so you can serve these whenever you like. The dipping sauce can also be used as a dressing for side dishes such as blanched bean sprouts or blanched spinach.

1 package small, square wonton wrappers
1 cup mung bean sprouts
1 pound ground beef
½ teaspoon salt

Korean Egg Rolls

Miss Sophie Lee at the Spotted Cat on Frenchmen Street, with Ted Long on bass

½ onion, chopped
2 green onions, chopped
3 cloves garlic, chopped
1 tablespoon fresh ginger, minced
1 tablespoon sesame oil
1 egg

Defrost wonton wrappers, if frozen. Blanch bean sprouts by dunking them briefly in boiling water. Let sprouts cool, then chop. Mix with beef and all other ingredients (except wontons). Place one teaspoon of filling in the middle of each wrapper, wet edges with water and fold wrapper over to form a triangle; pinch to close. Fry in vegetable oil on both sides until golden and crispy. Serve immediately.

**Dipping sauce**

Stir together:
2 green onions, chopped
2 cloves garlic, chopped
2 tablespoons Kikkoman soy sauce
1 tablespoon sesame oil
1 tablespoon roasted sesame seeds
1 teaspoon red pepper flakes

**IN THE KITCHEN WITH**

## John Autin

**PIANIST JOHN AUTIN SAYS IT TAKES A FEW EGGS TO MAKE GUMBO:** "I'm not a great cook by any means. I'm just a piano player. My wife is the cook in the family. But this particular recipe is something that I've done over the years and it's something that even a non-cook can do. I enjoy doing it because of that. I've been doing this particular recipe for 10 years.

Not being a cook, when you try to cook things, there is not a lot of reward. Usually you have to cook something several times before you learn how to do it. But this particular recipe came out really good the first time I did it, so it was very rewarding. And my wife loves it because she gets a break from always doing all the cooking.

If you just follow the recipe and do it exactly like she said, it comes out great. The variations on a gumbo are endless, but the basic thing that makes it a gumbo has to be there—the roux and the holy trinity. Once you have your own particular taste, you can use seafood, oysters, crab, or shrimp. You can put eggs in it.

Eggs in gumbo, I think of it as an Italian influence. They put them in spaghetti. After it's all done, you drop hard-boiled eggs in there. It doesn't really add any flavor; it's just something to have in there, in addition to everything. It's a variation on a theme. People put

**BORN**
1957 in New Orleans, Louisiana

**NEIGHBORHOOD**
Algiers Point

**INSTRUMENTS**
Piano, vocals, electric bass

**NOTABLE RECORDING**
"Don't Explain," *Piano Town*, 2011

**HOLY TRINITY**
Onion, olive oil, sea salt

all kinds of crazy things in gumbo. There's no one way to make a gumbo. I never had eggs in my grandmother's gumbo or anything. I had never had eggs in a gumbo before I had this one. Jill got this recipe the year before we got together. 1991. She's from Missouri, and she got the recipe before we even met.

The worst gumbo I ever had was in Sweden. They find out you're from New Orleans and it's 'Oh, you've got to try my gumbo! You've got to try my jambalaya!'

The worst ever was the jambalaya we had in Visby, Sweden, one day. It was pasta with Tabasco sauce and carrots. And then they go, [excited] 'What do you think?' [laughs] We were eating there because we were playing there with Anders Osborne. We were there for a month! People always want you to try their Cajun food wherever you are. It's amazing.

This is one of the best gumbos I've ever had, which is why I get a kick out of cooking it. My grandmother, Augustine Autin, she made one of the best. But everything she did was great. Redfish courtbouillon, jambalaya, crawfish bisque, all these things that take forever to cook. She lived in Houma, Louisiana. That's where my family's from.

One of these days, instead of chicken, I'd like to try a rabbit. In south Louisiana, I'm sure lots of people make rabbit gumbo, but we haven't done that yet. Also, smoked duck, I'd like to try that too."

## Yankee Gumbo

The original recipe came to John's wife Jill as a gift from Cynthia Broussard Fox in San Diego in 1991. Fox was born in Scott, Louisiana, and wrote at the bottom of her recipe: "If you are in a bad mood, tired, in a hurry, or want to impress someone with your cooking abilities, cook something else." The original recipe calls for one pound of okra, but since Jill doesn't like okra, John calls his version Yankee Gumbo: "This gumbo is pretty much my repertoire. It's the only thing I've cooked since we've been married, 15 years. If I can do it, anybody can do it."

(Feeds four Cajuns or six *Americains*)

2 quarts organic chicken broth
1 bay leaf
1 teaspoon black pepper
1 tablespoon Worcestershire sauce
3 pounds boneless, skinless chicken thighs
½ cup Teriyaki sauce
½ cup cooking oil (vegetable, corn, canola, etc.)
⅓ cup plus 1 tablespoon flour
2 onions, diced
2 bell peppers, diced
4 tender stalks celery, diced
2 cloves garlic, minced
1 pound fresh chicken andouille sausage
6 hard-boiled eggs
½ cup green onion tops, cut fine
½ cup cilantro leaves, whole

Pour broth into a large soup pot. Add bay leaf, black pepper and Worcestershire sauce. Marinate chicken thighs in Teriyaki sauce. Make the roux: Pour oil into a cold frying pan, add flour and stir with a flat wooden spatula until smooth; turn the heat on medium/low and stir constantly for 30-40 minutes until roux smells like popcorn and

John Autin calls his gumbo Yankee Gumbo, but you could call it Asian Gumbo, since it has Teriyaki sauce and cilantro

John Autin at Chophouse in the Central Business District

is medium brown. Immediately add onion, bell pepper, celery, and garlic to roux to cool it down, then add this to broth. Bring to a slow boil. Fry sausage over low heat to render out some fat. Cut into bite-size pieces and add to broth. Brown chicken (a few pieces at a time) in sausage fat, add it to broth as well. Simmer on low for about 1 hour. Turn off heat. Add whole eggs, onion tops, and cilantro. Stir and cover. Serve with rice.

## IN THE KITCHEN WITH

# Gia Prima

"If I want Italian food, I make it myself."

**BORN**
1941 in Roebling, New Jersey

**NEIGHBORHOOD**
Water, beach, and more water

**INSTRUMENTS**
Vocals, keyboards, drums

**NOTABLE RECORDING**
"I Want You To Be My Baby,"
*The King of Clubs*, Louis Prima,
Gia Maione, Sam Butera and the
Witnesses, 1964

**HOLY TRINITY**
Olive oil, garlic, onion

**FOR GIA PRIMA, NOTHING BEATS AN ITALIAN DINNER:**
"First of all, I'm Italian. I come from a beautiful Napolitano family that settled in the area of Trenton, New Jersey, in a place called Chambersburg. And that's where all of the Italians seemed to settle when they came to this country. My great-great-grandfather, Gennaro Chianese, was the founder of the Italian festival in Trenton. My grandfather, Joseph Maione, had the first Italian bakery in Chambersburg. My Uncle Gigi had the corner bar and grill in Chambersburg. My Uncle Louie had the meat and fresh produce market in Chambersburg, and my Uncle Stanley was the tailor. So I kind of sort of had it wrapped up. Food was a great part of their life, and I find myself the same way. I get my greatest enjoyment from a really good Italian meal. When I first got the job with Louis [Prima], he had an apartment at the Diplomat Apartments in Las Vegas, and on Sundays some of the band members, Sam [Butera] and the Witnesses, would go over to Louis' and somebody would cook something. So when I first got the job I said, 'Let me do it next Sunday.' So I went over and I fixed a pot of gravy with all the pork and the beef and the Italian sausage and meatballs and I served them supper and Louis said to me, 'You got the job.'"

And that's the way our life was. I cooked almost every night. Sometimes, we'd go out, but very rarely. And he just loved his food and his supper always had to be at five o'clock. I mean, five o'clock sharp! And then he'd take his nap after supper and wake up and go to work at the Sahara and the Sands and wherever we performed at the time, and that was his life. He loved it and he was very content within that realm. He was very scheduled for breakfast, lunch, and dinner.

Sometimes, he would fix breakfast for the kids and I. They loved daddy's biscuits. No special trick, not really. He used Bisquick, but he had the touch. They were so light and fluffy. They really were good.

Louis loved everything. Something that was always kind of special for him, and the kids were not fond of it, Pasta e Piselli, pasta with peas. It's a very common dish in Italian recipe books, but as a kid when my mama made it, I didn't like it so I didn't really pay attention to how it was made. This was Louis' favorite way of having it. After we got married, I started making it. It's a quick, healthy meal because you get your green vegetable along with the pasta. Nowadays, everything is broccoli, broccoli, broccoli. So this is a little different. Louis would like it about once a month.

When you're an entertainer you like to stay at home whenever you can, and of course when we had the children it was a good family time. The children loved the red gravies and the pasta. I would make a lot of veal Milanese, or veal Franscese. Milanese has Italian-seasoned breadcrumbs, and the Franscese is just lightly floured, that's all. And you serve it with a lemon, white wine, butter sauce. Milanese is like in New Orleans, paneed veal. If you have red gravy left over from one of your pasta dinners, you save it and put the veal under the broiler with a little bit of red gravy and mozzarella on top.

I'm living in Destin, and I think I'm the only Italian in the phone book for God's sake. There's no Italian deli here. They have a couple of Italian restaurants here but I don't go. If I want Italian food, I make it myself. It's not like New Orleans, loaded with the best of all kinds of food. I've settled for Publix grocery store. They're not too bad, but they're not authentic either.

When I was living in New Orleans all those years—I guess 18 years from the time Louis went into the coma until my parents became ill and I had sold Pretty Acres in Covington and settled the estate—I would take the kids to Panama City for the rides they had and I would pass through Destin. I started going, just overnight. I had a lot on my plate as Louis' estate was tied up for almost 20 years and had a lot of legal battles, so just to regroup and regain some strength back, I would come here for overnight and then drive back to Covington the next day. The drive, too, was therapeutic for me because it was peace and quiet and I really needed that. Always thought, some day I'd like to settle here, and after my mom passed I moved here in 2005. I'm not sure why I moved back here rather than to New Orleans, but if I ever move again, I'm going back to New Orleans."

## Pasta e Piselli (Pasta with Peas)

1 pound uncooked angel hair pasta
¼ – ½ cup olive oil
½ red onion, finely diced
2-3 cloves garlic, minced

Pasta with Peas, one of Louis Prima's favorites

Gia Prima and Louis Prima perform at the
Hotel Monteleone in the French Quarter in 1974

1 (15-ounce) can Le Sueur Peas
Red or black pepper, ground

First, boil salted water for pasta. Pour olive oil into a sauté
pan—at least a quarter cup because that's the only mois-
ture that's going to coat the pasta. Sweat the onion in the
oil and add garlic. Strain peas, discarding juice. Add peas
to onion mixture. Add pepper to taste. "Louis liked a little
red pepper." Cook pasta according to directions on box,
drain, then mix with peas. Serve hot.

Featured Prima photos and recipe used courtesy of
Gia M. Prima, Prima Music, LLC, and www.LouisPrima.com.

## IN THE KITCHEN WITH

# John Boutté

"My mom made po-boys with whatever my dad would catch."

**BORN**
1958 in New Orleans, Louisiana

**NEIGHBORHOOD**
Tremé

**INSTRUMENTS**
Vocals, cornet, piano, trumpet

**NOTABLE RECORDING**
"A Change is Gonna Come,"
*Jambalaya*, 2003

**HOLY TRINITY**
Shallots, garlic, bell pepper

**JOHN BOUTTE HAS FOUND WAYS TO IMPRESS FRIENDS THAT DON'T INVOLVE SINGING:** "The house I grew up in was actually built by my father and grandfather, and I can honestly say that it was built on po-boys. My mother would make the po-boys on Sundays, Saturdays. My dad would get his cousins and his friends and some beers. We came together as a community and built that house. We always had fresh produce. Beans and greens and lettuce, cabbage and roots. My great aunt was a true horticulturist. She had this beautiful bush, what they call ham and eggs, or bridal's wreath. And wonderful roses. You'd walk through those neighborhoods, man, you'd smell food and wonderful flowers. People did that because the streets weren't always that clean and they used their gardens as a bumper for the foul air of the sewerage.

My mom made po-boys with whatever my dad would catch. If there was no fish, she'd fry chicken livers. We had fried chicken liver po-boys, man. She fed a lot of kids and we ate well. Something we would beg for—this sounds a little gross—were brains, cow brains! We ate them for breakfast, man. She soaked them in cold water and took the membranes out, ran them through cornmeal and we thought we were eating oysters. It was delicious! Surprised I don't have gout. We'd have cow brains and scrambled eggs. Our brains wouldn't be scrambled because we always went to school with a full belly and well tanked up to attack the day. How she fed 10 children on a postman's salary? I don't know how, but she did.

My dad would go out fishing—this is how bountiful Louisiana was—he would go out fishing and catch so much fish, man. When he got tired of scaling and cleaning and stocking up, we'd literally give it away to the neighbors. My mama, she'd cook it, but she didn't want to clean no fish. And my dad would not eat fish unless it was right out of the water. So we had a lot of seafood in the house and we also had game because he was a hunter. We had venison and *cowan* [turtle], duck and *poule d'eau*—a little black duck—water hen is what it is, basically.

This is my stove. I looked it up and it used to be on cruise liners, and those stoves were built well, because you can't have a fire aboard no ship. Don't look, now. It's not too clean. Who's got time to clean their stove? Screw that!

This morning, I cracked two nice organic eggs and whipped them up really well and heated up the olive oil just right and slid it across there. There's something beautiful about seeing that egg go. Just flipped it over and put a little sour cream and parmesan and a little wheat toast. That was just quick. I like breakfast. In the morning, I'll do sweet potato pancakes. Instead of water or milk, I'll use—here's the trick—orange juice. And coffee. I drink coffee; coffee doesn't bother me.

I like the red wine too. Actually, I was in Colorado and doing a benefit for one of their public radio stations. Guy asks me do I like red wine? I said, 'Sure,' and he poured me a glass of this syrah and it was really good, and then he turned the bottle around and it was a bottle that was made in my honor. That was very humbling. I've done a lot of records and stuff, but to have your face on a wine bottle, that will really impress your friends."

## Glorious Oyster Pie

"You've got to make two, or everybody's going to get mad!" (Makes 2 pies)

2 deep pie crusts + 2 roll-out tops
4 tablespoons olive oil
4 shallots (or 2 small white or red onions), chopped
12 cloves garlic (about 1 head), minced
2½ stalks celery, chopped
1 teaspoon ground white pepper
1 teaspoon ground black pepper
1 teaspoon cayenne
2 pounds ground beef
1 teaspoon dried thyme
1 teaspoon salt
1 cup plain breadcrumbs
1 quart fresh oysters
1 bunch green onions, chopped
½ bunch parsley or cilantro, chopped

Sauté shallots, garlic, and celery in olive oil over low heat until soft. Add white and black pepper and cayenne. In a separate pan, brown meat, adding thyme and salt at the end. Add shallots, etc., to meat. Add breadcrumbs, oysters, and enough of the oyster liquor to make a soft dressing. As soon as the oysters start to cook (edges curl), turn the heat off. Fill piecrusts and cover pies with roll-

Glorious Oyster Pie

John Boutté at the St. Augustine Church
Christmas concert in Tremé, with Nobu Ozaki on bass

out tops. Stick a fork in the tops a few times. Bake in the oven at 350 degrees for 45 minutes. Serve with a dollop of sour cream.

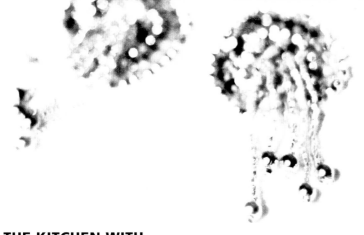

## IN THE KITCHEN WITH

# Trixie Minx

"Alcohol has allowed me to pursue higher education."

**BURLESQUE DANCER TRIXIE MINX SAYS COCKTAILS ARE ALL ABOUT THE SQUEEZE:** "I have a problem with wine. Once I find a wine I love, well, eventually it goes away. They only make so many cases in a year, so it's a constant hunt for that next beautiful bottle.

I started making cocktails in New Orleans because that's what everyone wants. Everybody drinks. I got into bartending because a friend of mine managed a bar in the Quarter. They were hosting the Playboy Mardi Gras party and had to have two female bartenders—it's in the contract—and they have to look a certain way. One of the bartenders got pregnant, so I had this crash course a week before Mardi Gras and learned how to make drinks. One of the playmates asked for drinks in baby talk, 'I'd like a grey goosey...' and that was bizarre—the best part of the party—communicating with that one, seeing her in action. She was a magical creature. I didn't exactly learn the art of making cocktails, but I learned the speed. I can swing a cocktail in under a minute.

Essentially, I don't like fruit. I like melon and bananas, but most fruits are too sweet. But if you cut them with alcohol, they're amazing! A little bit of fruit juice and a little bit of alcohol is perfect.

**BORN**
1981 in Miami, Florida

**NEIGHBORHOOD**
St. Roch

**INSTRUMENTS**
"I use thigh-high stockings as a guitar. They substitute for a banjo too."

**NOTABLE RECORDING**
"I have an act where I play 'Moonlight Sonata' on the piano, while I strip."

**HOLY TRINITY**
Milk, cheese, Tony Chachere's Creole Seasoning

They should work on infused fruit instead of infused vodkas.

We didn't drink much in my family. It was neighborhood block parties with margaritas and daiquiris, totally suburban fruity cocktails. I remember when I was five, maybe six, they gave me a virgin piña colada, and instead of asking the bartender for another one, I went around and took sips off of all the adult drinks. I got very cranky.

As a little girl, I had a very clear path in my head. Go to school, graduate, and become a ballerina. That's all I wanted to do. But then I broke my foot and I had an eating disorder, so it was a big mess. I have a cousin who's orthodox [Jewish]. Before his wedding, he asked me not to talk about my lifestyle. Keep in mind, this was before burlesque; I was just a cocktail waitress back then. [laughs] It was the alcohol he didn't want me to talk about, and it's funny, because now I really can't talk about it.

Alcohol has allowed me to pursue higher education. I was able to use all my cocktailing money and my bartending money to go to school and graduate. I hate to disappoint, but I'm sort of straight edge.

With as much cocktails as I make, my normal cocktail is actually whiskey and diet coke, or whiskey and water, sometimes whiskey and ginger ale. And if I'm feeling crazy—like, wild—I'll get a dirty martini. Just vodka. No vermouth. Just salty vodka. The funny part is that every time I perform with Comic Relief, all we drink is Jack Daniels. The New Orleans Bingo! Show is all Jameson, and with Fleur de Tease we drink Jim Beam. Backstage, they'll give you a certain amount of drinks for free or they'll offer to buy you a bottle. If you get one bottle it has to be the group choice, and from performing with these people for so long I've acquired a taste.

My Disco Lemonade recipe comes from bartending on Bourbon Street because there's always somebody who comes to you and goes, 'I don't know what I want. I'm not sure what I like...' and you have 20 people behind them who know exactly what they want, so you can't discuss the finer hints and notes and flavors. I discovered that if a drink is blue, anybody likes it. It doesn't matter what it tastes like; they just like the fact that they have a blue drink. And if you drink a lot, your tongue turns blue—and the more you drink, that becomes interesting in and of itself.

Then there's the Trixie-Tini, which I didn't come up with myself; it was made for me by Jamie Burton at the Royal Sonesta. Jamie actually created two drinks for me, both martinis. The Trixie-Tini is sweet and embodies everything feminine, and the Little Minx is spicy with hints of cinnamon.

Champagne is the drink of strippers. When I got married, I didn't register. We asked for gift cards to Home Depot and Lowe's—and don't ever do that. Register! If you don't register, people just get what they think you need and apparently everyone thinks that I need champagne flutes. I have eight different sets. I can go forever. If you ever need a champagne flute, please come to my house. Please! We should start throwing them into the walls at this point."

## Trixie-Tini

1¼ parts Stoli Vanil
½ part lemon juice
2 strawberries, puréed

Trixie-Tini, invented by Jamie Burton, bartender at Irvin Mayfield's Jazz Playhouse at the Royal Sonesta

Trixie Minx in her act "Idle Hand," set to "Big Toe" from *Party with Clowns* by the Clown Orchestra, with Fleur de Tease at One Eyed Jacks

Simple syrup to taste
Top with champagne
Serve with a fresh strawberry

## Blue Disco Lemonade

2 parts citrus vodka
1 part blue curacao
Top with equal parts lemonade (or sour mix) and soda
   water (or lemon/lime soda)
Serve with a lemon wedge

# IN THE KITCHEN WITH

## George Schmidt

**PAINTER AND BANJOIST GEORGE SCHMIDT CAN ALSO USE A KNIFE AND FORK:** "Painters mix stuff together, and you'll find a lot of painters who are cooks because it's an extension of this—instead of colors you're mixing flavors. I got myself Julia Child's *Mastering the Art of French Cooking*, but French cooking is like a mist before the eyes while Italian cooking is like a pat on the back. It's a bit more rational. French cooking, a lot of it comes from the Roman period. I've cooked Roman recipes. Ham *en croute* with figs—not quite up to speed in the modern sense, but good.

The Romans did what the French did later on. They specialized in taking a fish and making it taste like chicken, or taking a chicken and making it taste like fish. In other words, they were more interested in the trickery of cooking. You take the food and change it into something that it originally isn't. Quite frankly, I think the barbarian invasion of the Italian peninsula changed that, because the Germans were a little more practical. But the Romans liked trick food. Oysters that taste like ice cream—now, I'm kidding, but that's what they'd do. And this survives in some way in French cooking, especially desserts. Taking coffee and flaming it, for instance. If you go to Antoine's and get café brulot, that's an example of that kind

"I've had enough local cooking."

**BORN**
1944 in New Orleans, Louisiana

**NEIGHBORHOOD**
American Sector

**INSTRUMENTS**
Banjo, vocals, e-flat sousaphone

**NOTABLE RECORDING**
"Darktown Strutters' Ball," *Favorites*, New Leviathan Oriental Fox-Trot Orchestra, 2000

**HOLY TRINITY**
Tony Chachere's Creole Seasoning, Tiger Sauce, rosemary

of drama and theatricality of cooking that the Romans really pushed.

I lost my Julia Child's *Mastering the Art of French Cooking* because I had managed to crush a mouse in it. I don't know how that happened, but I opened it up one day and there was this flattened carcass of a mouse inside.

There's a local thing here, barbecued shrimp, and this is not that dish. This is a lot simpler. It has garlic, red hot pepper, thyme, and shrimp in it. That's all there is. The Creole method is to cook everything to death and to combine all sorts of stuff together—my friend used to call it Creole goop. There's a fusion of flavors. Italian cooking isn't like that. It depends upon the least amount of effort and the least amount of ingredients. At a certain age, you just can't keep going with all those creams and butters. You also have to cook something that doesn't take all day to do.

This I got from a recipe book that I have in here. My take on it is very simple. You always hear, 'serve with good, crusty bread.' But what I do is I make a toast out of this [Pepperidge Farm] whole-grain, whole-wheat bread. I find this has a sweetness that blends in with the shrimp taste, so that's my contribution to this dish. We'll put this on the bottom of the bowl and serve the shrimp on top because there's an enormous amount of juice that's created by the sautéing. The heads exude their goop and it creates a sauce, and after you eat the shrimp you eat the bread. People here do a lot of boiling, but all that flavor goes out into the water and you never get it.

I buy my garlic at the supermarket already peeled. And there's a thing that happens—have you ever had sauternes [wine]? Sauternes is made from grapes that are slightly turned; they call it the noble rot, and my garlic is slightly turned too, and there's a depth of flavor because of that. It's kind of like anchovy. But it gets cooked, and nobody gets the runs—so far.

I've had enough local cooking. My dad's 100 in June and he doesn't like anything anymore. He only likes his mother's cooking. My grandmother made her own noodles, and great roasts and gravies. Her gravies were like a perfume. They were so good you could inhale them. My dad says the old-time cooking is gone; he says it's all changed and I can see why, because the kids who go to culinary school learn to prepare food academically. It's not neighborhood cooking anymore.

A friend of mine came over for dinner and she doesn't like to eat with her fingers. She ate my shrimp with a knife and fork. I'm not recommending this, but it's an interesting experience. So that's how we do it now. We tell people, 'Go ahead and use your fingers, but we're going to use a knife and fork.' [laughs]

I serve this to everybody that comes here. There's no one who's escaped it. Even my Anglo-Saxon friend who doesn't like to eat with her fingers.

You don't want to eat shrimp uncooked. I have eaten uncooked shrimp. There was a sushi bar over here and I said, 'I want to try something I've never had.' Shrimp, served raw. It was like eating snot. Jesus! It was the worst thing I'd ever put in my mouth. Amazing what a little heat will do."

## BBQ Shrimp

¾ cup olive oil
1 head garlic, minced

BBQ Shrimp

Janet Heumann, George Schmidt, and Greg Merritt of the
New Leviathan Oriental Fox-Trot Orchestra
at the Mallory Society Ball

1 teaspoon thyme
1 teaspoon red pepper flakes
2 pounds fresh shrimp, heads on
1 teaspoon coarse sea salt

Heat oil in a large skillet. Sauté garlic, thyme and red pepper flakes for a minute. Add shrimp. Sauté over medium to high heat for 2 to 3 minutes; cover and continue to cook for an additional 2 to 3 minutes. Sprinkle with salt. Serve hot, with juice, over whole grain toast.

**IN THE KITCHEN WITH**

# Rick Olivier

"The way I see Creole is that you're free to improvise."

**BORN**
1957 in White Castle, Louisiana

**NEIGHBORHOOD**
Mid-City

**INSTRUMENTS**
Vocals, guitar, drums

**NOTABLE RECORDING**
"What I Know Now,"
*Shrimp Boots & Vintage Suits*,
Creole String Beans, 2011

**HOLY TRINITY**
Olive oil, onion, garlic

**RICK OLIVIER EATS CANE SYRUP TO HELP THE ECONOMY:** "I was kind of an afterthought in my family. My parents were both 43 when I was born and I have three older sisters. Consequently, my mom spoiled me. Did not have to cook for myself at all. Then I went to college and ended up getting really hungry. 'Wow, I have got to learn this,' and it didn't take long. Food is such a big deal here and my mom was just an amazing cook, but very classical Cajun country cooking the way it always has been done. I grew up in a little town called White Castle, which is an hour north of here, on the river. My dad would go hunting and get squirrels or rabbits or whatever, bring them home. My mom would cook them and we always had great food around the house. Not the healthiest food, because the Cajuns are into their fat, but I grew up eating some really good food.

We eat jambalaya all year round, a lot of gumbo in winter, and we eat a little lighter; I'm 52 now and I can't digest the roux like I used to. I'll make a little bit to put in the gumbo because you have to have it, but I do my gumbo more with okra and filé now. I love me some gumbo, but it's a cold weather thing for me. I'm big on the okra; I like okra.

Culturally, south Louisiana is just a goldmine. You grow up eating great food; you grow up hearing great music. It's all mixed up. The local music used to be played on AM radio all the time. The Irma Thomas, the Ernie K-Doe, you grew up hearing it. To me, it seems like a cool thing to play these songs—I just love these songs. All of the R&B stuff and the swamp pop. The guys in my band, we all realize that we really cannot write songs as good as Allen Toussaint and as good as Earl King, and we don't have time to learn and study that. Fortunately, the songs are already written. We just have to dig them up. Mix in the really well-known numbers with some obscure numbers. If people really haven't heard the obscurities before, then I don't think it matters that much whether you're playing original songs. I want to do the great songs, and I don't think we're going to run out of material any time soon.

Now, I want to make sure I don't cook something other than the recipe. Left to my own devices, I'll be throwing other stuff in. Who knows? I'd be putting some bay leaf or something.

My mom did not cook with cilantro—parsley only. You never saw cilantro in the supermarket prior to 1985, or 1979 maybe. I just happen to love the taste, but it also relates to this idea of Creolization. If something is Creole, it means that it's been adapted to the province. The way I see Creole is that you're free to improvise. It means that you can be in touch with the tradition, but put your own thing on it right now, which is cool. Anything that had parsley in it before, I feel totally free to use cilantro now.

To a lot of people, the idea of making shrimp-stuffed mirlitons is real exotic. But not to me. I grew up watching my mom make them. Stuffed artichokes, or whatever. They'd sit there, stuff the damn artichokes. It was just an everyday thing. But that is just very exotic to some people. My wife, the first date we ever had, I invited her over to eat with me and I made stuffed mirlitons with shrimp and she jokingly says that, well, that pretty much sealed the deal for her. They were good.

Our love for sweets in south Louisiana; you're in sugarcane country. And so, sugar is a big deal here. In my own hometown it was considered treasonous to not eat sugar. You ate sugar because you were surrounded by sugarcane fields. It was good for the economy. I love sweets. I have a terrible sweet tooth. This is the most traditional Cajun dessert ever. Steen's is the brand that I like, Steen's cane syrup, and you don't clean the plate off or anything. You put some of this on your plate and then you take your sliced white bread—this was my dad's favorite dessert, he ate it every night—and there you have it. It's called syrup and bread. It's good too."

## Creole String Beans

"These are not your five-dollar bag of pretty beans. Real snap beans."

1 (14-ounce) pack smoked beef sausage
1 yellow onion, chopped
½ red bell pepper, sliced
1 stalk celery, chopped
3 cloves garlic, chopped
½ cup fresh chopped cilantro
1 large Creole tomato, chopped
½ jalapeño pepper, chopped
1 tablespoon Worchestershire sauce

Creole String Beans

Creole String Beans (the band) at the Rock 'n' Bowl

1 teaspoon sea salt
½ teaspoon black pepper
Juice of 1 lime
1 tablespoon Steen's cane syrup
½ cup Chimay ale
1½ pounds fresh string beans

Slice and brown sausage; remove from skillet. Add seasonings (onion through jalapeño) and sauté for 10 minutes. Add sausage back in along with Worchestershire, salt, pepper, lime juice, cane syrup, and ale. Simmer for 15 minutes and stir to prevent sticking. Add string beans.

Stir, cover, and simmer to your preferred "doneness." If mixture begins to dry out, add a splash more of Chimay. Serve over rice.

## IN THE KITCHEN WITH

# Barbara Menendez

"I'm 50, and I get how to do this."

**BORN**
1960 in New Orleans, Louisiana

**NEIGHBORHOOD**
Uptown

**INSTRUMENTS**
Vocals, keyboards

**NOTABLE RECORDING**
"You," *16 Songs Off A Dead Band's Chest*, The Cold, 1984

**HOLY TRINITY**
Onion, olive oil, cracked black pepper

**BARBARA MENENDEZ IDENTIFIES WITH THE HELP—AND NOT JUST ONSTAGE:** "My son Weston, who is also in my band [the Help], he put it to me this way about cooking. He likes to cook because I've always cooked, and I said to Weston, 'You know, one day, everything that you've ever learned about cooking just gels, and it's like an epiphany.' And he goes, 'Like jazz!' and I'm like, 'Exactly! It's like the day you understand jazz.' I love how he said that. Basic cooking is like building a foundation for any structure in the construction business. You can build anything on top of it. You just need to know how to make a solid foundation.

The cooking I do, I guess it's indicative of New Orleans. Low and slow. People ask me to make gumbo, debris, stews. I make jambalaya too, a white jambalaya with chicken—thighs have the most flavor—and you fry them, take them out, and then into the fat you throw tons of onion and some bell pepper, cover and cook that down for 20 minutes, and then you add your dry rice into the juices that came out of the vegetables and cover and let that cook for a while; then you throw in the sausage. I like andouille sausage for everything. I heard, 'You never put andouille in red beans,' but get out! Andouille's the best. Then you put your chicken back in, add water and then garlic at the end. If you sauté garlic, it pales too much and loses its punch.

[Meowing] That's my cat in there, sequestered. She actually can't come out because she'll jump up here and put her face in the crawfish. She'll put her face in your sandwich, and she'll go, 'Oh, hi, thanks.' I love her to death, but my biggest fear is getting hair in the food.

I make my roux fast. You start when you're 20 doing it low and slow because you're terrified, but I'm 50, and I get how to do this, and I'm not going to burn it, and I'm not going to be here forever. The other thing I do is I use olive oil. The earthier the dish, the more I prefer olive oil. When you start your roux, just ignore it for a minute. If I start spazzing about it, it's like watching water boil; it never happens. So just wait. But once it's hot, you've got to pay attention because it turns quick.

I first made this recipe when I was pregnant with Weston, and he's 27. I originally got it from Justin Wilson. I don't believe recipes, usually. It's art; it's a spiritual thing. You're adding your own love, your own stuff. People should just relax when they're trying to cook, get their own channel going. Emeril, who I love dearly, his whole 'kicking it up a notch'—I'm sorry. Everything doesn't need to be kicked up. Creole cooking is a lot subtler than that.

The first thing I ever learned to cook was red beans and rice from Dolores Tillman. I call her my mom. I was born in 1960 and grew up in Lake Vista, which was sort of the Northshore of those days. Dolores came to work for my mother when I was 10 months old, and she worked for my mom for 23 years. I used to pull my chair up and watch her cook. She was from Honduras, had nine children of her own, helped my mom raise her seven. The way she makes red beans is how I make red beans. Basically, you chop everything big and throw it in the pot. You don't soak your beans overnight, you just cook it for four hours until it becomes this creamy goodness. A half stick of butter, a pot spoon of ketchup. Onion, garlic, carrots, pickled pork—I put andouille sausage. But now, I brown my vegetables first, and they're not only great, they're amazing. It's just that extra bit of love that makes the difference.

My mom cooked. Well, she tried. That's mean, but she had Dolores. She didn't have to; Dolores cooked. Dolores did everything. She always made red beans and rice on Monday, and the best fried chicken in the world! It's just salt, pepper, flour, and chicken, but the secret is that the oil has to be fresh and you shake the excess flour off, don't let it get gummy or anything. Wash the chicken, cut it up in pieces, sprinkle it with salt and pepper—generously; I'm heavy-handed like her. And she'd get a big brown grocery bag and put flour in there and throw that chicken in there and shake it up—genius. I told her, 'You've got to be lying to me,' and she said, 'No, baby. That's it.'

When did I last see her? Was it a year ago? Yes, it was. Because I go by my weight. Like a year ago, September. There's an SNL skit called 'Cooking with the Anal Retentive Chef.' He'd chop up something and end up putting it in the garbage because it wasn't perfect and then he had to get it ready for the garbage. I do that. In little Ziploc bags, so it won't stink. [Holds up bag, zipping it shut.] See, isn't that nice? [laughs]"

## Crawfish Stew

3 pounds Louisiana crawfish tails
1 tablespoon salt

Crawfish Stew

Barbara Menendez fronts the Help at the Hi-Ho Lounge,
with Rich Siegel on guitar

1 teaspoon black pepper
½ teaspoon cayenne pepper
1 cup olive oil
1¾ cup flour
8 cups chopped Vidalia onion
¾ cup chopped celery
1 bunch parsley, leaves only, chopped
¾ cup chopped green bell pepper
1 jalapeño, seeded and chopped
¼ cup (1 head) chopped garlic
4 (8-ounce) bottles clam juice

Season crawfish with salt, black pepper, and cayenne pepper. Prepare roux, using olive oil and flour, a dark chocolate brown. Turn heat down and add onion, celery, parsley, bell pepper, and jalapeño. Sauté for a few minutes. Cover and simmer over low heat for 1 hour until it becomes a bubbly ooze (periodically scrape and stir so it doesn't burn). Add seasoned crawfish and garlic, cover and simmer for 20 minutes. Add clam juice and keep cooking over low heat for up to 1 hour. Add more salt to taste. Serve over rice.

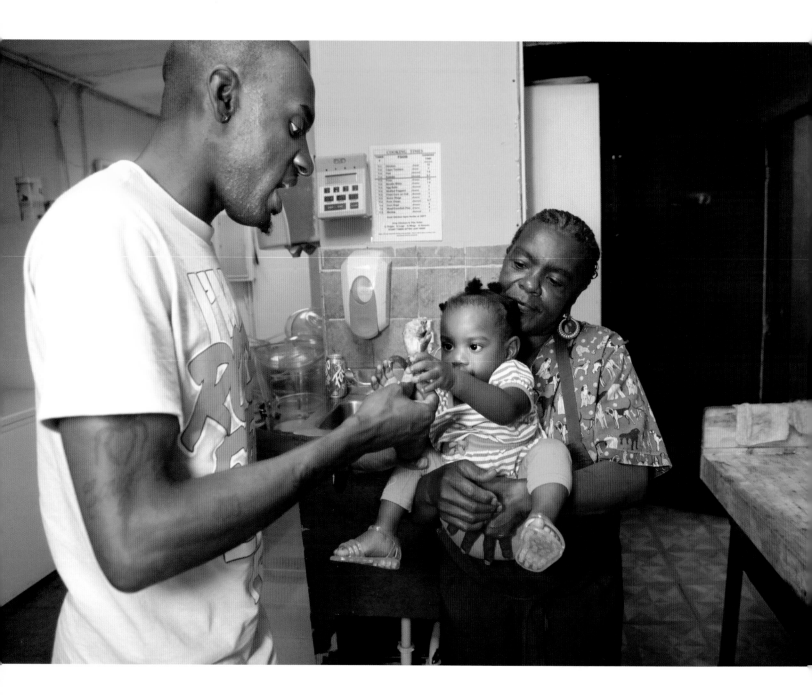

**IN THE KITCHEN WITH**

# 10th Ward Buck

**MARLON HORTON, A.K.A. 10TH WARD BUCK, DROPS AND GIVES US FIFTY (WINGS):** "I like hot. I like to use Crystal because I've experienced it and it's not too salty. Some hot sauces have their own taste.

Men love spice. My Mardi Gras [sauce] is not too hot, where my women are starting to take onto it also.

We call it the Mardi Gras sauce because it has a little bit of everything. On the float, they throw the beads but they also throw teddy bears. You're not going to get just one thing. You want the spice, you want the sweet, you want it all. If you're human and you're getting beads around your neck, you're going to want the cayenne and the honey mustard and all that.

Since this is the best sauce we have, I wanted to call it something that's real familiar with people. I experimented in the restaurant I had before this, Lucky Buck's on the Westbank, that a friend and I opened after Katrina. That's how I knew this would be a hit. We were selling sandwiches and red beans and all the stuff I know how to cook at home, but when I got into chicken, that became our best seller. Then we were like, 'We'll open a wing shop.' It's cheap, and your overhead is low.

*"I don't have to use somebody else's. I can do my own."*

**BORN**
1980 in New Orleans, Louisiana

**NEIGHBORHOOD**
St. Thomas

**INSTRUMENTS**
Vocals, trumpet

**NOTABLE RECORDING**
"Make It Jump,"
*The Definition of Bounce,* 2011

**HOLY TRINITY**
iPhone, Lucky Johnson, God

Zatarain's taught me to put the water on, do this, do that. On the package, it tells you step by step. And I was like, 'Hold on, this is real simple. Let me start making my own. And when I eat stuff, I know what's in it. If I don't know what's in it, I know what the taste is. If I found something I liked, I'd mock it and try to do the same thing. I don't have to use somebody else's. I can do my own.

I was going to Delgado. I went to cooking school because I wanted to enhance what I was doing. I could have trained up to be a chef, but I had my own restaurant [already] and I didn't have time. So I switched my major to business management. Everybody in that program wanted to run their own restaurant and I already had my own.

I just found out how good a cook my mama is. The cook of the family was my auntie, until she passed away. She would do the gumbo, that's the number-one-selling food in my family. Gumbo! So we'd be by my auntie's all the time. Then, when she passed away, my mom took that role.

My grandmother is from Talladega, Alabama, and we're from New Orleans. When we went there and saw her doing this and that to the animals, we were like 'Ew, that's gross, we don't go after our own animals!' I stopped eating crawfish for a while because I took the kids crawfishing and we had to take a piece of the crawfish tail and throw it back in, while it was still alive. For the family reunion, when they put the crabs in the pot, I walk off. If it's a rat, you kill it, because that's what we're taught to do. Roach—kill it. But not the pig, and all the little animals we saw on Sesame Street.

One time, we went and caught this fish and brought it home and I added some seasoning and I fried it and my cousins, they was licking their fingers. 'Brah, who put this together?' I said, 'Me, man.' 'Where you get this from?'

'We caught it.' [fakes choking] That's my family. They didn't like the fact that I'd caught it. I waited until they finished eating, and they was licking their fingers, that's how I knew I had something, because fish is real simple and basic. You can't put too much on fish. When I put that fish together, I knew I had something. So I started doing red beans and fish, macaroni and fish, everything and fish, until I got this chicken idea. And chicken goes with everything. Some of my sauces, we try putting them with the pork chop, and it don't work. I've got to get to that theory. But chicken, you can put it in anything.

I fry my chicken wings for nine minutes. What we do is, we drop 20 [frozen wings] and pre-fry them for about seven minutes, so you have some already ready. And when the customers come, you drop them two additional minutes. They shouldn't be here more than four minutes waiting for their food.

Growing up in New Orleans, sometimes you don't have a lot of food in the house, so you experiment with what you have. You take the salt and add it to the pepper; that was the first that everybody did. Then I noticed cayenne, and we put cayenne in everything. I started experimenting with different ingredients. Some were nasty, some were good, some were like winners, so we stood with the winners. When I opened my wing shop, I put about 40 flavors out and 30 of them won. We thought we were going to have between 10 and 15, but it was hard to knock certain ones off.

I learned this. If I'm putting pepper in the lemon pepper, then I'm killing the lemon pepper. I'm killing the lemon in the lemon pepper. So you don't want to mix things that are the same. If I'm mixing fruit punch, I don't put orange with orange, you want to add your apple, your banana, all that."

Wings covered in Mardi Gras Sauce

10th Ward Buck hosts his first political rally at Marlene's Place on Tchoupitoulas Street, running for City Council District B, with dancers Milton Adams and Broderick Smith

# Mardi Gras Sauce for Wings

2 cups honey mustard salad dressing
4 tablespoons Crystal hot sauce
2 tablespoons Weber Kick'n Chicken seasoning
1 tablespoon cayenne pepper

Mix everything together. Serve. (The salad dressing should be mayo-y and quite sweet in order for the recipe to come out right. If you use Kraft dressing, replace 4 ounces of the dressing with 2 ounces honey and 2 ounces mayo.)

# IN THE KITCHEN WITH

## Helen Gillet

"Potatoes saved the day, yet again."

**BORN**
1978 in Leuven, Belgium

**NEIGHBORHOOD**
Upper Ninth Ward

**INSTRUMENTS**
Cello, loop pedal, electronics, vocals, drums, E.V.I.

**NOTABLE RECORDING**
"Waking Milo,"
*Running of the Bells*, 2011

**HOLY TRINITY**
Onion, garlic, ginger

**HELEN GILLET DETAILS THE SUBTLE CONSIDERATION BEHIND A PROPER BELGIAN FRY:** "I was born in Belgium and my family is from Verviers, which is very close to where the fry originated. It started in the Meuse Valley—the Meuse is a river in Southeastern Belgium—but the origin of the fry is from 1680, which is before Belgium was even a country. Poor inhabitants of that area used to cook up small fish from the Meuse River, fry them. But when the river froze over, a woman grabbed a potato and cut it into long shapes that resembled the fish and threw them in the fryer. It's still a Belgian tradition to have these thick fries. This is the Belgian way. Of course, fries have gone all around the world and the French fries tend to be skinnier.

The secret to the Belgian fry—and there really is a difference; in Belgium everyone celebrates how good these fries really are; there are fry stands all over Belgium and you go there; they serve them with all sorts of dipping sauces, which I'll talk about in a minute—but you fry them twice! The first time on a lower heat, until the fry is barely cooked all the way through, for 5-10 minutes. I don't have a fry-daddy or a *friteuse* with a basket inside, which is really what I'd need for this, because it has a temperature gauge, so I'm using my gumbo pot. Let the fries cool completely and then right before serving, you fry them again on a very high temperature for 3-5 minutes until crisp and golden.

God, it's so loud! I'm imagining what it was like for women to make fries for their families during the war. Belgium was a very bloody battlefield during World War II and potatoes saved the day, yet again. Fish and chips? Total steal! Everything, when it comes down to it, really originates in Belgium. The Smurfs are from Belgium, I'd like to point out. Those little adorable blue creatures, called Schtroumphs in French. They originated in a very similar location to where the fry originated. So, yeah, a lot of good things coming out of Belgium. Glad to share.

Let's discuss the stages of the fry. We're at stage one: the raw fry. Some of these are better cut than others, but we did find one of the more perfect fries here. And I think we're ready. I'm now placing the fries in the pot and you'll hear a change in the sound. Aaah, the fryer is happy; it has its fries. I'm using a safety device between me and the oil. Some people call this a strainer. I like to think of it as a fry-safety device. It's good not to get your skin too close to the hot oil. So, we get it all in, and now I'm going to monitor them. It's like being a lifeguard. And we're going to have a sip of beer, which is also a very Belgian thing to do.

I learned how to make fries in Belgium from my friend Louise-Marie and her mom. I never paid attention more than when I was at the *fritures* themselves, waiting in line for fries, and you just see it happening. Another thing I've failed to mention is to salt the fries right away when they come out of the fryer the second time. It's important not to wait because you want the salt to absorb into the hot oil. Otherwise it falls off. Remember, you want the fries to cool completely before you cook them the second time.

You can leave them on the counter or put them in the fridge. I've never tried freezing them, but I don't see why that wouldn't work. The shock effect of going from cold to hot helps. Another trick for cooking these fries in New Orleans is to turn your AC up really high.

If you were to go to Chez Antoine in Brussels and order fries, you would have your choice of different colored forks—green and pink and blue and white and yellow and orange—so you get your choice of what you're going to eat your fries with, and you let them know what sauce you want, and the sauce is crucial. A true Belgian fry-eating experience is about a mayonnaise-based sauce. How you make your mayonnaise is going to affect how you enjoy your fry. I learned how to make mayonnaise in Belgium. It's very simple. You take an egg yolk and a teaspoon of mustard—this is Louise-Marie's mom—and you slowly pour the oil in while you stir in one direction and it's important to keep stirring in the same directions because otherwise it might not take, solidify, have the right consistency. Today I'm doing the quick and dirty, which is putting some [store-bought] ketchup and mayonnaise together, and we're going to call this cocktail sauce.

Now the fries are ready to come out. Feel the fry. It must be cooked almost all the way, just barely cooked! The worst thing in the world would be to bite into a fry that's not cooked all the way through, but you also don't want them to fall apart. These look good; these look real good, actually. But this one is mushy and this one is teaching me that I need a *friteuse* in order to treat people to an even better Belgian perfection.

Fries are like crepes. You can put anything you want on them. I've been thinking about a dipping sauce with blue cheese and avocado, but I haven't tried it yet."

Helen enjoys her Belgian fries at home in the Musicians' Village with mayo mixed with ketchup, straight mayo, and mayo mixed with fresh garlic

Helen Gillet plays on the sidewalk in the Marigny, during a cover shoot for the February 2010 issue of *OffBeat* magazine

# Belgian Fries

Large russet potatoes (about 2 per person)
Vegetable oil or peanut oil
Salt
Ketchup
Mayonnaise
1 clove garlic

Peel and wash potatoes. Cut them into half-inch thick fries. Deep-fry in oil for 5-10 minutes until fries are barely cooked. Let fries cool completely. Fry fries again in oil for 3-5 minutes until crisp and golden. Salt fries immediately. Serve hot with mayonnaise-based dipping sauces of your choice. Helen always serves a "straight mayo." She also stirs together equal parts mayonnaise and ketchup for cocktail sauce, and minces a clove of garlic and stirs it into mayonnaise in a third bowl for "fake aioli."

**IN THE KITCHEN WITH**

# Leroy Jones

*"Potato salad in gumbo, I like doing that."*

**BORN**
1958 in New Orleans, Louisiana

**NEIGHBORHOOD**
Tremé

**INSTRUMENTS**
Trumpet, flugelhorn

**NOTABLE RECORDING**
"Melancholy Serenade,"
*Sweeter than a Summer Breeze,* 2009

**HOLY TRINITY**
Garlic, onion, bell pepper

**LEROY JONES PREFERS OKRA WITHOUT THE SLIME:** "To be honest, I don't really know where I learned to cook, except that I just started doing it. I guess, subconsciously, I was paying attention and didn't realize it.

I make a mean black bean. Yes, indeed. Any kind of bean, that's one of my specialties. Red beans and rice, black beans, black-eyed peas, white northerns, limas, baby limas, anything you want this side of the downtown area.

We're not into using recipes. Occasionally we'll get a recipe and we'll doctor it up to our tastes, desires, and requirements. In preparing New Orleans food, everyone has their own way of doing it and it's like improvising in jazz—you can do it any way you want just as long as it swings.

Today, I'm making smothered okra. Fresh or frozen, it doesn't matter. Sometimes you can't get fresh okra and sometimes you can. I take the okra and I pour about four tablespoons of white vinegar over the okra in the saucepan and the acid from the vinegar absorbs a good 85 percent, maybe more, of the slime. I prefer okra without the slime. The dish will be almost done, just about 98 percent completed with the cooking, before I put the shrimp in. That way they don't get hard and don't shrink up too much.

One thing about me when I cook is I keep an eye on my food. I think that's the key to having the food come out better and not get burnt. I can't be on the phone or running outside. Get out and have a conversation with the neighbor—'Oh, my food! Forgot it was even on.' We rarely burn food around here.

I keep my workstation pretty clean. Everything is in order. I use a small cutting knife to mince my seasonings; onions, garlic, bell pepper—anything that I'm chopping up. The big knife is great and is probably more efficient, but I think that I've developed a certain technique where I can get through mincing a whole onion or bell pepper in less than 60 seconds. I've snipped a bit of my fingertip and it's easier to do that with that big butcher knife because it's got so much weight on the handle. Never bad enough to go to the hospital or anything like that, but after that happened I left the big knife alone. For me, using a small cutting knife is much safer and easier on my nerves.

When I was a child, gumbo would be our main entrée. My mom would fix the gumbo and then you would have potato salad as a side.

Potato salad in gumbo, I like doing that. Some people think 'Blech! That's crazy.' I like it. If the gumbo is real spicy, the potato salad kind of cools your mouth off. You've tried that? There are even New Orleanians who won't be that adventurous. 'You can't put your potato salad in your gumbo.' Sure you can! Good flavor."

## Smothered Okra

"The vinegar absorbs the slime from the okra. Believe me, your food will not taste like vinegar, as you will find out! It won't taste like a salad."

1 green bell pepper, minced
1 yellow onion, minced
2-3 cloves garlic, minced
3 tablespoons extra virgin olive oil
1 pound okra, sliced
4 tablespoons white vinegar
1 pound fresh shrimp
1 (8-ounce) can tomato sauce
3 teaspoons sugar
½ pound turkey smoked sausage, sliced thin
3 bay leaves
Tony Chachere's Creole Seasoning
1 teaspoon filé powder

Sauté bell pepper, onion, and garlic in olive oil. In another pot, sauté okra in vinegar for 5-10 minutes. Peel the shrimp and put the heads and shells in a third pot with 4 cups of water, bringing it to a boil and letting it simmer for 5-10 minutes, then strain the stock. Add tomato sauce and sugar to seasonings (bell pepper, etc.) as well as okra, shrimp stock, smoked sausage, and bay leaves. Simmer for about 1 hour. Season with Creole Seasoning to taste. Add peeled shrimp and simmer for a few minutes. Turn the heat off. Add filé. Serve over rice.

Smothered Okra

Leroy Jones at the Norwegian Seamen's Church, with Steve Pistorius on piano

# Maple Cream

This is a simple dessert that Leroy Jones' wife, trombonist Katja Toivola, makes.

4 eggs
1 cup maple syrup
3 cups warm milk
Pinch of salt

Preheat oven to 350 degrees. Whisk eggs. Add maple syrup, warm milk, and salt. Pour mixture into ramequins and bake in a bain-marie until mixture sets, about 45 minutes. Let cool and serve at either room temperature or refrigerated. Stays good for several days in the fridge.

## IN THE KITCHEN WITH

# June Yamagishi

*"I like complicated stuff."*

**JUNE YAMAGISHI IS ALWAYS IN SEARCH OF SAUCE:** "In Japan, we eat the golden-fried pork chop, *tonkatsu*. I don't make that. I use a soy-sauce base that is fruity and sweet, with apple, ginger, and honey. This is the secret: sake makes it sweet; makes meat tender.

When I'm in a restaurant, I always sit at the bar to see the cook and learn. Camellia Grill, they cook inside the counter and I like to sit down and stare.

When you grind your ginger, don't peel it. With the skin you get more flavor. John Gros can cook too. His gumbo is excellent, and we always gather, once every year, at John's house and bring a dish. I bring golden curry, curry with rice. Not Indian curry. My curry is Japanese style. More close to stew, with chicken, beef, or pork, whatever you like. I don't put much mushroom. I put onion, carrot, and potato. Onion is most important. Cooking the onion first, about 20 minutes, make it caramel brown, kind of make it shrink. I use this sauce mix, Japanese roux, 'Golden Curry,' and I put carrot chunks, potato chunks, put the water and boil for one hour. Before that, put seasoning stuff. Salt and pepper, and I use Tony Chachere's a lot. When I do beef, I fry the beef in butter first. When I add the water, I add the beef back in.

**BORN**
1953 in Ise City, Mie Prefecture, Japan

**NEIGHBORHOOD**
Lower Garden District

**INSTRUMENTS**
Guitar

**NOTABLE RECORDING**
"Darlin' You Know I Love You,"
*B.B. King & Sons, Live*, B.B. King, 1990

**HOLY TRINITY**
Soy sauce, Bull-Dog Vegetable & Fruit Sauce (Semi-Sweet), Tony Chachere's Creole Seasoning

My secret ingredients are this fruit sauce [Bull-Dog Vegetable & Fruit Sauce, Semi-Sweet] and this Japanese version of Worcestershire sauce, with tamarind. You can put it on steak, anything. Give it secret flavor.

Let me tell you my story. I was moving down here in 1995. Around that time, not many Japanese people lived here in New Orleans. I couldn't find Japanese groceries, this kind of sauce stuff. And I wanted to eat it. I wanted this kind of flavor. I make it. Worcestershire sauce and ketchup, mixed up. That's close.

When I go back to my home town, there's a butcher close to my house. I always go there and get the fried beef croquettes. I love it! That's my favorite. Ground beef with mashed potato, carrot, onion—same as for curry, but chopped up. Put together and put breading, panko, and deep-fry. I'm from a town close to Osaka, and Osaka is the food capital in Japan, like New Orleans. Anything is great, and cheap! I've been eating beef croquettes since I was two years old.

I learned to cook from my *grand-mère*. First time I get here and eat the red beans and rice, it reminds me of my *grand-mère*'s cooking. She always used the red beans. That's why I moved down here. Because of my *grand-mère*'s red beans.

I started cooking when I moved to New Orleans. Makes me feel like cook. I cooked when I lived in Japan, but mostly I cooked New Orleans stuff; gumbo and jambalaya. When I moved down here, I really started cooking for myself: 'Yeah, let's cook this!' But I don't need to cook gumbo and jambalaya here. I cook in the Japanese style.

My hometown Ise is by the sea with a lot of great seafood and special beef. Best beef in Japan, better than Kobe beef. Unbelievable; melt in your mouth. Ise shrimp, Ise *ebi*, is very good. I always hung out by the sea and the river as a kid. That's familiar to me.

I like deep-fried shrimp. Shrimp cutlets, like Tiger shrimp. Peel it, open it and stretch out, like tempura, golden-fried with panko. Then I put this sauce, the fruit sauce, with mayo, mixed together.

I like complicated stuff. Complex stuff is crab cream croquettes with the bechamel sauce, your white sauce. That's very hard to make. I try and try and try—still can't make it. They're too soft, they won't make a chunk. You chill it in the refrigerator to make it more firm, then you cut it and deep-fry in panko. Outside flaky, inside creamy. That's a problem. Just bechamel sauce and crab meat. Very hard! When I put it in the oil to fry, it breaks. Too soft, I guess.

Jason [Mingledorff] wrote a song and we were in Colorado before we cut the second album with Papa Grows Funk. We stayed in a condo, everybody. 'Yeah, let's cook something.' 'Hey, June, can you cook the *yakiniku?*' Like Korean barbecue. 'I'll do that. No problem. Bring me to some store.' But I couldn't get *yakiniku* sauce, so I had to make a temporary sauce with soy sauce and sake and sugar. And then Jason said, 'Hey guys, what do you think about this song's title?' I said, 'What about the *yakiniku?*' And that was it. And then I put the ingredients in the liner notes."

## Japanese Pork Chops

1 tablespoon grated fresh ginger
1 small apple, grated
2 tablespoons honey

Japanese Pork Chops

June Yamagishi with Papa Grows Funk at Tipitina's

2 tablespoons mirin
4 tablespoons sake
6 tablespoons soy sauce
2 center-cut pork chops
Salt
Black pepper
Tony Chachere's Creole Seasoning
½ cup flour
2 tablespoons olive oil

In a bowl, stir together ginger, apple, honey, mirin, sake, and soy sauce. Set aside. Season pork chops with salt, black pepper, and Tony Chachere's on both sides and press into flour in a wide bowl. Fry pork chops on both sides in olive oil over medium heat for about 3 minutes per side, covering pan with a lid after the first minute. Pour sauce over meat and continue to cook for 2 minutes, turning the meat in the sauce.

## IN THE KITCHEN WITH

# Lars Edegran

"I don't use curry powder."

**BORN**
1944 in Stockholm, Sweden

**NEIGHBORHOOD**
Lake Vista

**INSTRUMENTS**
Piano, banjo, guitar

**NOTABLE RECORDING**
Soundtrack for *Pretty Baby*, 1978
(ABC Records) nominated for an
Academy Award for Original Music Score

**HOLY TRINITY**
Fresh curry leaves, whole cumin seeds,
ginger

**WHAT ELSE WOULD WE EXPECT FROM SWEDISH PIANO PLAYER LARS EDEGRAN BUT INDIAN FOOD?** "When I came to New Orleans in the '60s, I didn't know how to cook anything. I actually learned to cook while I was living in New York—that's when I got into this Asian cooking. How I got interested, that goes further back to when I used to go to England, before I came to America. I really liked the Indian food there, and then I met my wife who is from England, and we were going out to a lot of curry restaurants.

I've been cooking Asian food for over 20 years. The technique is very important when you cook Asian food. Everything has to be in the right order; you have to cook onions to a certain degree that I did not know about before. Also, certain ingredients like fresh curry leaves. Fortunately, I have a next-door neighbor who has a curry plant in his yard! I had a curry plant too, before Katrina, but the plant died and the guy next door said, 'Don't worry, I'm going to plant one.' And they are much better gardeners than I am anyway. He got the plant going and it's becoming like a tree. So any time I need a few curry leaves, I just go over there and snap a branch off.

You use the curry leaves when you first put your oil in the pan. Heat the oil up and throw the curry leaves in there and this incredible aroma comes out of the pot. The curry leaves flavor the oil. You don't actually eat the curry leaves; they're like bay leaves. It's the same with the whole spices, cumin seeds or whatever you use; you fry them in oil also and they flavor the oil, which then flavors everything else in the dish. Those are the things that I've learned. And it's made a big difference in my curries.

Most Indian chefs don't use curry powders. They mix their own because each recipe has a different mixture. Most of the things I cook, I don't use curry powder. I just mix cumin, coriander, turmeric, whole cinnamon, and cardamom.

I cook some Burmese and Thai dishes. I make my own green curry paste with cilantro and dried shrimp paste and my own red curry paste—but I'm not really an expert on that. It takes a long time to make, but then you can keep it in your fridge forever.

When you're cooking Indian food, chopping and cooking the onions takes up the most time. Once it gets cooking, you don't have to watch it so much, but the early preparation takes a lot of time. You'll be standing there. But it's fun. I just put some music on. I enjoy it.

I started cooking New Orleans food when I was up in New York. I got some of Paul Prudhomme's cookbooks. I lived in New Orleans, in the French Quarter, from 1965 to 1979 and then I moved to New York. I started cooking jambalaya. The reason I cooked it in New York was because I wasn't in New Orleans—I could not get it, you know. But since I moved back here, I have not cooked gumbo because that's an elaborate thing to cook. I guess Indian food is elaborate too, it's true, it is, but I'd rather learn more about the Asian cooking. I'm going to try some other Asian things now, I've decided. I'm going

to try some different lentil dishes, black-eyed peas with mushrooms, vegetable dishes I haven't tried, and I'd like to try a korma. I've never cooked a korma, it's a cream-based curry dish. Shrimps in coconut milk with chilies and curry leaves—that sounds great, too. Sesame-seed lamb chops, I tried that the other day. It came out really good. You make a marinade with yogurt and lemon rind and the meat becomes very tender—you tenderize meat with yogurt. I was amazed. And here's a recipe for lamb kabobs. I can't wait to try that. Meatballs! In creamy cashew nut sauce. I would rather do those than the Swedish meatballs because I like a little more spice.

Learning about Indian cooking, I've had a few flops. You can't do what you do in some European type of food, where you add spices at the end. You can't do that in curries. That's a total flop then. Dried spices have to be fried in the early process. Otherwise, the dish doesn't taste right. Also, you don't want too much liquid, that can become a flop too. And don't worry about using too much oil because you can always take it off at the end. But if you don't use enough, then the food doesn't come out right. Because it's the oil that flavors all the food."

## Madras Chicken à la Lars

Edegran finds his dried spices (and occasionally, fresh curry leaves) at International Market in Metairie.

4 tablespoons vegetable oil (or more)
2 teaspoons whole cumin seeds
10-15 fresh curry leaves
2 big onions, finely diced

Madras Chicken à la Lars

Lars Edegran at Preservation Hall, with Richard Moten on bass

½ head fresh garlic, minced
1 thumb-sized piece fresh ginger, peeled and minced
6 tablespoons madras hot curry powder (Rajah brand)
1 teaspoon hot chili powder or cayenne (optional)
6 pounds chicken drumsticks
2 (15-ounce) cans tomato sauce

Pour oil into a deep frying pan. Add cumin seeds. Heat until seeds start to pop. Add curry leaves. Cover immediately and lower heat. After 30 seconds, uncover and add onion. Cook onion down until brown (not black) over low heat for about 30 minutes, adding garlic and ginger about halfway. Then, add curry and chili powder, adding a little hot water if food sticks to the pan. Add chicken and brown on both sides. Transfer chicken to a large casserole dish. Add tomato sauce to what is left in pan. Bring to a simmer. Pour sauce over chicken and bake in the oven, uncovered, at 350 degrees for 30 minutes, and then at 300 degrees for 90 minutes. Turn chicken pieces over after 1 hour. Serve with basmati rice.

## IN THE KITCHEN WITH

# Big Al Carson

**BIG AL CARSON EATS HIS VEGETABLES:** "I grew up right here in New Orleans. I'm homegrown, as I always say. I grew up in the Seventh Ward and the Lafitte projects. I'm right here in the midst of things. Homegrown.

I used to cook more than I do now, because I just can't stand up at the stove like I used to. And cooking is a hands-on thing. If you want it right, you've got to stand there, cultivate it, you know—make it what you want. But I do have some favorites I make. I love to cook cabbage. I like to smother it down with pig tails and ham hocks. I like it real smothered down, where it lays over the rice real nicely. You don't have to break it up no more, once you get it from me. And there's one dish I don't think anybody else does: it's zucchini and squash, with shrimp and smoked sausage. It don't take long. I don't have a name for it, I just do it. It always comes out right for me. Of course, I'm a hot sauce man, so I have to throw a little hot sauce in there. I love Crystal—there's nothing else. I have nothing against the others, but Crystal's my favorite. It has a nice little tang.

Some people like tomato sauce, and some people don't. I like the tomato sauce, so I throw a can of whole tomatoes in there, with the

"A regular Creole family; we ate red beans and rice every Monday."

**BORN**
1953 in New Orleans, Louisiana

**NEIGHBORHOOD**
Central City

**INSTRUMENTS**
Vocals, tuba, trombone

**NOTABLE RECORDING**
"Take Your Drunken Ass Home," *Take Your Drunken Ass Home*, 2002

**HOLY TRINITY**
Hot sauce, garlic, onion

juice. Just to get some acid in there, because zucchini is sweet, so you've got to put a little tart in there.

I'm a sea salt man now. I've been trying to lose weight, and I have, so I don't use anything but sea salt—the brown sea salt, not the white sea salt. The brown sea salt doesn't have as much sodium content to run your pressure up.

I serve my squash over noodles. I like shells, I don't know why. You can put it over fettuccine, that's good too, but my personal favorite is over shells. And don't overcook them!

This dish is something I kind of made up trying to impress my first wife [laughs]. Did it work? Yeah, it did. So I've been using it ever since. I keep on making it. I made it for my second wife. That worked too. Even better! We've been married four years this November, but we've been together 16 years. Now, she cooks! My wife is Spanish, from Honduras. She cooks very well, and her mother, my mother-in-law, lives with us, so I ain't missing no meals. She cooks leaner than Creoles or black folks cook. The culture is different, and she sticks with her culture. We eat all fresh, and I prefer that now. We don't eat corn out the can, we don't eat peas out the can. Maybe some string beans once in a while, but most everything is fresh. That's the way we do.

When I was growing up, my younger sister did most of the cooking. She's a fantastic cook. My mom cooked a lot, but you know, mom worked a lot too, so my sister always took over. A regular Creole family; we ate red beans and rice every Monday. You knew you was going to have spaghetti on Wednesday. Friday was always fish, trying to adhere to the religious thing, but we weren't religious in that aspect, it was just a cultural thing. Seafood on Saturday, but it was all fried; fried fish, fried this, every-thing was fried. The smoked sausage was fried. I haven't had a hot sausage sandwich in so long, I dream about it sometime. Trying to stay away from that kind of stuff. Your body changes, and the hot sausage don't sit on you like it used to. That was one of my favorites. I used to play at a club called Fourth Edition and this little guy, Speedy, was a cook. One day I asked him, 'Make me a Big Al Special.' And he said, 'What?' I said, 'Take that hot sausage and deep-fry it, then take it out, cut it open, and put it on the grill. Put it with some grilled onions, some American cheese, and mayonnaise, mustard and ketchup, and hot sauce, and lettuce and tomatoes, and extra pickles.' That's a Big Al Special. On French. Oh, God. I can taste it now! [laughs]

I used to go to Norway. One of my best home-cooking experiences was in Norway, when I stayed with someone and not in a hotel, and this couple could really cook. One dish she did was lasagna, and it was just stacked. The ground meat was so real. The next morning when they left for work, I had to call them and say, 'You want any more of this lasagna? Because I'm going to kill this for breakfast!' But when I came back a couple of years later, they'd upset my world. They'd turned vegetarian on me! Vegetarian lasagna! With eggplant! Oh, shit."

## Creole Squash

1 pound Bryan's smoked sausage
1 onion
1 green bell pepper
2 tablespoons olive oil
2 yellow squash

Creole Squash

Big Al Carson at the Funky Pirate Blues Club on Bourbon Street

2 zucchini
4 tablespoons butter
1 cup broth, water or white wine
1 (14½-ounce) can whole tomatoes
1 pound peeled shrimp
1 teaspoon Tony Chachere's Creole Seasoning

Slice smoked sausage about 1-inch thick. Chop onion and bell pepper and fry, with sausage, in olive oil. Slice squash/zucchini into 1-inch thick chunks and sauté in sausage mixture with butter for 5 minutes. Add liquid and the can of tomatoes, breaking up the tomatoes a bit with a cooking spoon. Season with Tony Chachere's and simmer, covered, for 10-15 minutes. Add shrimp and cook until they turn pink. Serve over pasta shells.

**IN THE KITCHEN WITH**

# Sean Yseult

"Now, where did the thyme go?"

**BORN**
1965 in Lemoore, California

**NEIGHBORHOOD**
Lower Garden District

**INSTRUMENTS**
Bass, piano

**NOTABLE RECORDING**
"Black Sunshine," *La Sexorcisto: Devil Music, Vol. 1*, White Zombie, 1992

**HOLY TRINITY**
Olive oil, garlic, parsley

SEAN YSEULT LEARNED TO COOK IN NEW ORLEANS: "This was my dad's skillet, and the only thing he left me in his will. He was an English professor and writer, so he didn't have a lot to leave any of us. It was actually very sentimental, because he was also a great cook and used this skillet once or twice a day for decades.

When I toured with White Zombie I was a vegetarian. I became a vegetarian in high school because I got a scholarship for ballet and I lived on campus and I didn't trust the food. I wasn't strict—I'd eat a can of tuna sometimes—but I didn't have money to eat in restaurants. Then I go to New York. We lived on the Lower East Side, and there were so many places you could eat for 75 cents. You'd get a falafel, a slice of pizza, or a cream cheese bagel, lots of coffee, that kind of vegetarian. Just street food.

When I moved here 14 years ago, I started making jambalaya right away. I was obsessed with it, and I've always made it with brown rice. Nobody's complained. Locals, believe me, they're like, 'No way that's brown rice!'

[To quail:] That looks crowded enough. They're having a little party in there. Next time I'm going to lay them with all their feet the same way so it'll be like Busby Berkeley; a formation dance.

I always read the food section of the *Times-Picayune*, read the recipes and clip a few and try things out. I do the shopping and when I go to the store, every single thing I buy is for something, and then I see Chris [Lee, from Supagroup] pulling out the asparagus: 'No, no, put that back! I need that!' So I get possessive over just about anything. He gets possessive about meat.

We make a serious breakfast. I roast asparagus and then I crack an egg on top and grate some gruyere on top of that, put it back in the oven and let the egg bake. I do a lot of eggs and vegetables in the morning, and if Chris is in charge there'll usually be some bacon or sausage also.

I make a beef orange stew, but you have to make it three days in advance. You keep taking it out and heating it up and adding stuff and refrigerating it overnight. It's French; I like French cooking. I make a roasted chicken with 40 cloves of garlic where you blanch the garlic; keep the skin on and boil it in water for 10 minutes. Fry the chicken up in some olive oil, a little thyme, then add all that garlic all around it, put a lid on it and cook it for 40 minutes. Take the chicken and garlic out and deglaze the pan with a little white wine and butter and you have a sauce.

My dad was quite the cook. He taught me how to make marinara sauce, and before he passed away he got really into bolognese. That I've tried, and really mastered. I'm really proud of my bolognese sauce. I used to think it was just a meat sauce, but there are all these steps where you let it absorb different liquids, almost like risotto. One time is white wine, one time is milk, and it takes hours, but it's worth it as long as you have a lot of people coming over to appreciate it. I watched my dad make bolognese in this

skillet. He loved Italian cooking, and I do too. For Chris' and I's wedding, we got some amazing Italian cookbooks.

Now, where did the thyme go?"

## Reindeer Gumbo with Quail

Sean Yseult and Chris Lee get reindeer sausage by mail from his parents in Anchorage, Alaska.

**Spice mix**

1 tablespoon salt
2 tablespoons dried basil
2 teaspoons paprika
½ tablespoon dried mustard
½ tablespoon chili powder
½ tablespoon garlic powder
1 teaspoon cayenne
1 teaspoon cumin
1 teaspoon black pepper
½ teaspoon white pepper
½ teaspoon thyme

**Gumbo**

3 pounds semi-deboned quail
1¼ cup flour
8 tablespoons olive oil
1 large onion, chopped
1 large green bell pepper, chopped
1 red bell pepper, chopped
2-3 stalks celery, chopped

Sean Yseult stacks her quail in a neat pile

Sean Yseult with Rik Slave and Rock City Morgue
at One Eyed Jacks

7 cups chicken broth
1 pound reindeer sausage or andouille
4 cloves garlic

Rub spice mix onto quail. Pour leftover spice mix into flour, mixing well. Lightly flour quail and fry in 4 tablespoons oil, browning both sides. Remove from skillet and set aside. Add remaining oil and flour into skillet. Make a 4-minute roux over high heat. Roux will look a yellowish brown from the start because of the spices, but try to make it a bit darker. Add onion, bell peppers, and celery, lower heat, and stir for 5 minutes. Heat broth separately, then add vegetables to broth along with sausage and garlic. Simmer for 45 minutes. Cut each quail into four or eight pieces, add to pot. Simmer for 15 minutes. Serve over brown rice.

## IN THE KITCHEN WITH

# Eric Rogers, Ryan Rogers, and Michael Girardot

"I enjoy cooking large quantities of meat."
—Eric Rogers

**BORN**
1986 in Marrero, Louisiana

**NEIGHBORHOOD**
Marrero

**INSTRUMENTS**
Drums, vibraphone

**NOTABLE RECORDING**
"I, the People," *Shock and Awe*, Sam Sarah, 2005

**HOLY TRINITY**
Onion, garlic, bell pepper

**WHAT DO MEMBERS OF INDIE ROCK BANDS DO WITH TIME OFF? THROW A POTLUCK:**

Eric: I am eating breakfast, which is leftover hibachi. Filet mignon for breakfast, with scallops.

Michael: I had Cheerios.

Eric: I learned to cook by just watching other people. Ryan has been in the fine dining service industry for over seven years.

Ryan: Ten years now.

Eric: Jesus! Well, he's always whipping up stuff around the house, and our dad always brought home fresh fish. Our stepfather is a big grilling guy and I took to that more than baking or sautéing.

Ryan: You cook on the grill rather than on the stove.

Eric: I enjoy cooking large quantities of meat. A long time ago, a friend of mine had a party at his parents' house, and I was craving ribs. I had never made ribs and I was like, "I think I can do that." So we made a whole rack of beef ribs and everybody was raving about these ribs. They're really simple, nothing complicated about them, but from that point on I was "Eric Rogers, the rib guy." People kept asking me to do them.

Ryan: I make the classic Creole sauces. Hollandaise and bechamel and reduction sauces, or red tomato sauces, *sauce tomate*. I do the simple stuff. Beurre blanc—white wine and butter and lemon juice—is the quickest thing in the world.

Michael: I came up with a large family. My mom's method of cooking was looking in the refrigerator, seeing what we had, and in about 20 minutes she would have the whole family fed. I also learned a lot from my grandma, who cooked a lot of food in large quantities. A few years ago, we started throwing potlucks at my house. It's a good way to have a lot of people over, have a party, and it doesn't cost us a lot of money. We do it about once a month and it's been going on for at least two years. I started making my grandmother's corn pudding recipe for these potlucks and at this point, if someone comes to a potluck and there is no corn pudding ...

Eric: ... it's a letdown. It's quite the dish.

Michael: It's really easy, but people seem to dig it so I keep making it.

Ryan: I'm going to make a red cabbage and green apple coleslaw and add some ginger and call it Asian.

Michael: Aren't you making something else as well?

Ryan: Just a roasted vegetable medley. Potlucks in the past, I've tried to go a little too gourmet on the crowd.

Eric: One time, Ryan comes late and brings baked pears with bacon and cheese on them.

Ryan: No, it wasn't bacon. Prosciutto.

Eric: Oh, excuse me. Anyway, the kids and the uncultured palates didn't like the prosciutto. Like me. There's been hits, and there's been misses. The ribs that didn't turn out as good as others were ribs that were rushed. The best ones I've made I probably cooked for seven or eight hours.

Michael: I like putting a bunch of stuff in a pan and putting it in an oven. King Ranch Chicken is another dish. There is no ranch [dressing] in it. I think the name refers to a ranch. Basically, it's chicken, a lot of cheese, tortillas, peppers, and Rotel tomatoes.

Ryan: Our step-dad is from Lafayette, so he has a Cajun side to his cooking.

Michael: Tell the story of the deer, at your dad's house.

Ryan: My dad hit a deer. It wasn't destroyed and we don't like to waste things, so we prepared the deer. I made deer roast and paneed deer.

Eric: It was a lot of deer.

Ryan: He hit the front quarter, but the back of the deer was still in mint condition. Fed a lot of people with that deer.

Michael: My kitchen is okay. But Ryan brought his own shredder and tongs and his own knife and knife sharpener and his own whisk.

Eric: And you brought salt!

Michael: He brought his own salt.

Eric [to Ryan]: Who doesn't have salt? I'm insalted!

Michael: Hosting a potluck, most of the work involves cleaning up your house so it's presentable. The great thing about corn pudding, I've gotten to where I can make it in about five minutes and stick it in the oven, which is great, when you're trying frantically to make your house presentable and be a good host.

"Most of the work involves cleaning up your house."
—Michael Girardot

**BORN**
1986 in Austin, Texas

**NEIGHBORHOOD**
Broadmoor

**INSTRUMENTS**
Keyboards, trumpet, vocals

**NOTABLE RECORDING**
"Rocketship," *Hey Kid*,
Big Rock Candy Mountain, 2009

**HOLY TRINITY**
Mushrooms, crazy salt, meat

Eric Rogers and Empress Hotel at Tipitina's

Ryan Rogers and Empress Hotel at Tipitina's, with Jack Clark on keyboards

## Cajun Ribs

5 pounds meaty beef ribs
5 pounds meaty pork ribs
Salt and black pepper
Paul Prudhomme's Meat Magic
1 (quart) jar Jack Miller's Barbecue Sauce
1 tablespoon ("butt-load") Tabasco
1 bottle beer (Coors Original)
12 ounces spicy brown mustard
⅓ cup maple syrup
¼ cup Worcestershire sauce

Start the day before the party. Season ribs with salt, pepper, and Meat Magic. Mix remaining ingredients into a marinade. Marinate ribs overnight in a covered container. The next day, line a cookie sheet with aluminum foil. Lift ribs out of the marinade and place on cookie sheet. Bake at 175-200 degrees for 6-8 hours. Pour marinade into a saucepan and reduce it to about half. When ribs are ready, slather in warm sauce. Serve immediately.

Michael Girardot and the Revivalists at Voodoo

Cajun Ribs and Corn Pudding

# Corn Pudding

1 stick butter
2 (14-ounce) cans creamed corn
2 (14-ounce) cans whole kernel corn
1 (8-ounce) box Jiffy corn muffin mix
4 eggs
½ cup light brown sugar
2 tablespoons honey

Heat oven to 350 degrees. Melt butter in a 13" x 9" Pyrex pan in the oven. Drain one can of whole kernel corn (leave liquid in the other one). Pour all ingredients into pan and mix with a fork until well blended. Bake for 45-50 minutes, until pudding wiggles like jello and no longer sloshes around.

## IN THE KITCHEN WITH

# Renard Poché

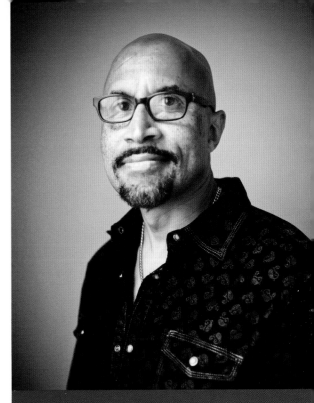

**RENARD POCHE IS STILL IN THE PROCESS OF PERFEC-TIONATIN' LEMONADE:** "I don't exactly have a name for this, but I guess we can call it a citrus fruit cocktail. How this came about is I've always liked lemonade, and a few years ago I went through a really bad time, so I was looking online for natural antidepressants. Citrus fruit was high on the list: citrus, salmon—even salt. I thought salt and sugar were depressants, but according to the research I did more recently, I found that a little salt can lift you. And actually, this has worked. I don't know if it's the power of suggestion, but it does. I had a few losses: my mother had passed, my daddy had passed, my brother had passed. Just a whole lot of stuff. When it rains it pours, and this was soon after Katrina. Hard times. So that's what led me to this. I've been doing it for over a year now and I think it's fruitful—eh, I didn't intend that.

I keep a supply. I fill this container, which is probably 64 ounces. When it runs out, I do it again. I'll go through it in two days, three days sometimes, depending on what's going on. Then I make another one. If I'm too lazy, or just don't have time to do it, then I'll just eat an orange straight up. So I'm consuming citrus fruit just about every day. This is like a pleasure food for me. If I'm in the

**BORN**
1956 in New Orleans, Louisiana

**NEIGHBORHOOD**
Old Jefferson

**INSTRUMENTS**
Guitar, bass, drums, percussion, keyboards, trombone, trumpet, flute, recorder, vocals

**NOTABLE RECORDING**
"I Got Some Funk 4 U," *4U/4Me*, 2009

**HOLY TRINITY**
Spring mix, bell peppers, walnuts

studio practicing, I'll have a 16-ounce glass like this and sip on it; might do two of them.

I'm kind of an old-school guy in a lot of ways. I had the manual citrus juicer. But when I lost it, I got this electric one, and I get a lot more juice out of the fruit now.

My sister has tasted this, and the keyboard player in my group, Keiko. She came over—we were rehearsing, or as Dr. John would say, 'We was rehearsalin"—and she liked it a lot. This is nothing fancy, just a version of lemonade. I'm still vacillating, kind of experimenting, with what I prefer. It's a little smoother with more orange balancing out the bite of the lime and lemon. Makes sense, right?

I want to get the perfect mixture. I write it down sometimes. Sometimes I do two oranges, one lemon, and one lime, depending on availability. I'm going to sweeten this with stevia extract in the liquid form. My sister and my brother-in-law thought it was too sweet, so I backed off the stevia and found that I really enjoyed it more because now I'm getting more of the taste of the fruit. Stevia extract has alcohol in it, 11 percent. I mention that to anybody who's going to try it because maybe they can't do alcohol for some reason. It's not much, but I still feel like I should mention it.

I saw an acupuncturist once and he said you shouldn't use ice, and I didn't ask why because I assumed it was for your heart. My mother had a heart attack once and she said they told her not to drink anything too cold. So I try not to use ice, if I can. I try to have the state of mind to keep everything in the refrigerator.

I eat simple. I don't have many guests. Like my sister visiting, she said, 'Renard, all you eat are nuts and berries.' Breakfast, five or six days out of the week, this is what I eat [taking packets of frozen fruit out of the freezer].

Dark cherries, blueberries, all these dark things are high in antioxidants. And it's good to have fruit on an empty stomach, otherwise it ends up fermenting in the tract somewhere. It's always fruit for breakfast. If I don't do the berries, I'm doing peaches or apples or banana, that kind of thing. But two hours later, I'm eating real food. I have a fast metabolism, so I eat five or six times a day. I eat a lot of whole wheat pasta, or spinach pasta, and salmon. Also, I'm a bachelor and I like sardines. I bought seven packets last night, and in two weeks they'll be gone. I eat salad with the yellow, orange, and red peppers, grape tomatoes and spinach, romaine and assorted greens, then I'll add walnuts and dried cranberries, olives, and I'll pour some of the olive juice on it. Quick and easy. I always like the dark vegetables because they have more nutrients.

My parents cooked, but it was more like soul food. Occasionally now, I'll eat soul food. Fried chicken, that might happen once or twice a month. The philosophy I follow is that 85 percent of what I eat is good. The other 15 can be bad."

## Citrus Cocktail

2 large lemons
1 large orange
4 large key limes (or 1 lime)
1½ quart water
½ teaspoon stevia extract (or 6 envelopes stevia powder)

Juice citrus. Add juice to water along with some pulp. Sweeten with stevia. Enjoy cold in a tall glass.

Citrus Cocktail

Renard Poché at the Ogden Museum of Southern Art
Photo by Golden G. Richard, III

## IN THE KITCHEN WITH

# Wanda Rouzan

**WANDA ROUZAN'S WEBSITE CLAIMS SHE'S NOT JUST "A TASTE OF NEW ORLEANS" BUT "A WHOLE MEAL":** "When we came back after Katrina, we decided that we needed some social life. The city was so dead. Nine of us, all relatives, decided we'd buy Saints season tickets once the Saints were coming back, and then we started a poker group because we all played poker. My parents played poker. My mom was in several clubs; my dad ran the poker at the Wonderful Boys Club; and at the Autocrat Club my uncle ran it, so there's history. We learned young. So the Friday night poker group kind of got revisited. It's all cousins and a couple of friends in the neighborhood. We alternate houses and we fix nice dinners and play cards. We play dealer's choice—wild cards up the yang yang—I mean just having as much fun as you can.

　After I found out yesterday that the meeting was here at my house, my sister had bought shrimp—we're Catholic, so we don't eat meat in Lent on Friday—and she said she felt like stewed shrimp, shrimp Creole as people call it. And then our youngest sister, she's flying in as we speak, she always likes boiled crawfish; she's spoiled, she's the youngest. Every time she comes in we have to have what she wants. And I said, 'Let me pick up a couple of cans of crab meat,' so I just

**BORN**
1947 in New Orleans, Louisiana

**NEIGHBORHOOD**
Gentilly

**INSTRUMENTS**
Vocals

**NOTABLE RECORDING**
"I'm Gonna Sit Right Down & Write Myself A Letter," *A Taste Of New Orleans*, 1989

**HOLY TRINITY**
PAM, olive oil, butter

made a crabmeat casserole, and a potato salad. You can't have shrimp and crab without potato salad, that just goes with it, and green peas, and carrots, and my sister is making a fresh green lettuce and tomato salad. And bread pudding! That's my idea of dessert.

The harder and staler and crustier the bread is, the better. Nutmeg is the favorite of all my spices. I use lots of nutmeg. I love to cook. I can be exhausted when I come in from teaching all day, and I'm going to cook. It's relaxing to me. In my next life, and maybe even in this one, when I retire from teaching, I've always wanted to become a chef.

We came from a cooking family, of course. My father was the main chef. He cooked almost all Sunday meals, all special occasion meals. So I would always be in the kitchen with him, making sure I always got the best parts, and then of course I started chopping seasonings and making gravies. My first gravy was a white gravy that was supposed to be a brown gravy, but I didn't brown my roux enough. But it tasted good, so I learned. I love gravies, over some rice with some veal, or stewed chicken, or hen, and I love stuffings. I love oyster dressing, just love making it, and it always goes.

I'm known for the savory dishes, not the sweets. I like to cook the long gravies, and my gumbo'll make you hurt yourself. Long dishes, as we call them. Pot food.

I started learning from my daddy, watching him, and also from the neighbors. You were everybody's child. The lady who lived across the street, Ms. Leda, would always be cooking something. She was one of the elders in the Boutté family, Lillian and John and all of them. She was one of the good ol' Creole cooks. My aunt made a fried potato po-boy to die for! These were the old-time dishes. My daddy-made an oyster soup, and my momma made codfish balls. And we always had boiled spaghetti with a nice tomato gravy, and always lettuce, tomato, avocado, and cucumber salad, almost every day of our lives. We grew up eating good food, poor man's food, and every Good Friday my daddy took us either crabbing or crawfishing, and we'd come back and sit up underneath the carport and boil crabs, boil crawfish, whatever we had—a seafood boil. When he went hunting we had duck, rabbit, nutria, and coon. My sister didn't eat that, but I ate everything. He'd cook all that wild stuff. *Cowan* [turtle], he'd go clean the *cowan* in the backyard and come in and cook that.

I'm a fanatic about cooking clean. I hate to come behind people, and my daddy was a terrible dirty cook, he didn't clean nothing; he left it all for his daughters and his wife. So I'm a clean cook. By the time I'm finished, my counters are clean."

# Bread Pudding

4 eggs
1 (12-ounce) can evaporated milk
1 cup milk
2 teaspoons vanilla
½ teaspoon salt
1 teaspoon cinnamon
1 teaspoon nutmeg
½ teaspoon allspice
2 cups light brown sugar
1 stale loaf French bread, sliced
1 (14-ounce) can condensed milk
1 stick butter
1 (1½-ounce) small box raisins

Bread Pudding

Wanda Rouzan at Xavier Prep, with Mark Brooks on bass
and Roderick Paulin on tenor sax

In a bowl, mix eggs, evaporated milk, and regular milk with a fork. Add vanilla, salt, spices, and brown sugar. Place bread into a deep 13" x 9" pan. Melt ¾ of the butter and pour over bread along with ¾ can condensed milk. Add raisins. Pour milk mixture over bread. Set aside in refrigerator for 1 hour. Add remaining butter in small clumps on top, along with the last of the condensed milk. Bake at 350 degrees for 45 minutes.

## IN THE KITCHEN WITH

# Debbie Davis

**DEBBIE DAVIS GETS ALL STEAMED UP:** "I don't think I ever did learn to cook, honestly. I just made up a bunch of stuff as I went along. It's something I started doing out of necessity. Either because I was trying to impress somebody or because I created small people who were hungry, and I was obligated to feed them.

I started making baked ziti with my mom; it's a New Jersey thing. Baked ziti is almost more popular than lasagna in Jersey and I'm not sure why, except that you don't have to be as patient with the pasta. Plus New Jersey is crawling with Italian people. I'm not one of them, but I grew up with them. Lots of Irish and lots of Italians—lots of Catholics—and they all like to eat and drink. Some more than others. Lots and lots and lots and lots and lots of cheese. More than two pounds of cheese in this dish, which I'm not apologetic about at all. I'm not shy with the garlic either, especially in the wintertime, because it keeps me from getting sick. I may smell awful, but I'm healthy and awful. Healthy and stinky is fine with me.

Both my kids are under the age of seven so they're both kind of picky. I started making different dinners for everybody. I got over that real quick. Now I try to make sure there is at least a side dish the kids can eat, so they'll eat that, and then try the thing that I'll make

*"Not being afraid is what happened."*

**BORN**
1974 in Queens, New York

**NEIGHBORHOOD**
Tremé

**INSTRUMENTS**
Vocals, ukulele, kazoo, tambourine

**NOTABLE RECORDING**
"Everything Right is Wrong Again,"
*It's Not the Years, It's the Miles,* 2012

**HOLY TRINITY**
Garlic, butter, salt

them try that I know they're not going to like, because you have to try it at least once.

If you can find it, if you can muster it, if you can grow it, if you can at all do it—fresh basil. I keep a pot in the window of my kitchen and I kill it often, by being me. I can keep mammals alive, plants not so much. My dogs always live past their 15th birthday, my kids are in the 90th percentile for height and weight, but I can look at a plant sideways and kill it.

My oldest son is six and in kindergarten, thank God. My youngest is two and a half. My kids eat a lot of peanut butter and jelly sandwiches in school. I don't think I could keep people alive if not for peanut butter. If you've got a peanut allergy you're going to die on my watch.

I try to cook things I can use more than once. Make enough, so there's another meal we can get out of it. I'm big on the leftovers, big into cooking once and eating twice. Because honestly, there are so many other things I need to do.

I cannot say this enough—don't overcook the pasta! In fact, undercook it. It should be less than al dente, so it's thirsty when it goes in the oven. Otherwise it won't absorb the sauce, and it'll be past ready to eat when you take it out.

I learned the starts of this recipe when I lived in Jersey, but I didn't start refining it until I got here. Not being afraid is what happened. Not being afraid to experiment and use more spices. Jersey can be a puritanical development, so it can be a bit tame, a bit conservative. In New Orleans, the motto is 'If less is more, imagine how much more more would be.' There is no shame in going a little bit too far.

I like cooking, I think, primarily because when I'm in the kitchen everybody leaves me alone. I can listen to music and I don't have to find a toy or a tooth or whatever else has gone missing. Oddly enough, there is sanctuary in the kitchen.

Really good cheese I like to splurge on. Romano, parmesan, asiago, any of the exotic Italian cheeses. And by exotic I mean expensive. Don't get that shit in the jar. If you get that shit in the jar, you may just as well not eat. The stuff in the green can. It's cheese food, it's what they feed cheese. It says right on the can. No thanks.

I use my hands. It might seem unsavory to some people, but they don't wear out, they don't need to be sharpened, and they always do exactly what I tell them to."

## Baked Ziti

2 handfuls fresh spinach, finely chopped
1 (15-ounce) tub ricotta cheese
2 tablespoons (or more) minced garlic
½ teaspoon salt
1 teaspoon black pepper
4 tablespoons (or more) grated Romano cheese
1 pound uncooked rigatoni or ziti
1 quart red sauce (whatever you like, homemade or not)
1 dozen fresh basil leaves, finely chopped
1 pound shredded mozzarella

Combine spinach, ricotta, garlic, salt, pepper, and half the Romano in a small mixing bowl. Cook pasta according to directions on package, but undercook it by 2-3 minutes. Drain, rinse with cool water, and return to pot. Add red sauce and basil to pasta, combining thoroughly, while adding mozzarella a handful at a time as you mix. (Save

Baked Ziti

Debbie Davis at Three Muses, enjoying a Muse gin cocktail
with cucumbers, strawberries, and elderflower liqueur

two fistfuls of mozzarella and the rest of the Romano to sprinkle on top.) Now for the "dumping, scooping, and splashing" stage: Grease a deep pan or casserole dish, about 12 x 8 inches. Put a thin layer of pasta evenly across the bottom, then a thin layer of ricotta mixture. Next you can add a layer of sautéed eggplant, or cooked fresh sausage, if you like—such as the Italian sausage from Terranova's on Esplanade.) Add another layer of pasta, then another layer of ricotta. Finish with a layer of pasta. Top with remaining cheese. Cover loosely with tin foil and bake in the oven at 350 degrees for 45-60 minutes. Remove the tin foil after 30 minutes and continue to bake

until the edges start to brown and the middle is bubbling. Let stand for 10-15 minutes before serving.

## IN THE KITCHEN WITH

# Mystikal

**BORN**
1970 in New Orleans, Louisiana

**NEIGHBORHOOD**
Uptown

**INSTRUMENTS**
Vocals

**NOTABLE RECORDING**
"Shine," *Unpredictable*, 1997

**HOLY TRINITY**
God, family, black pepper

**THE RAPPER PICKED UP COOKING TIPS IN PRISON:** "I do most of the morning cooking. I'm the breakfast chef. I grew up in New Orleans, Uptown, in the 12th Ward, a block off of Louisiana and a block off of Tchoupitoulas. My mom cooked everything. Gumbo, all the traditional New Orleans cuisine; the red beans, the crawfish étouffée. She got down, from the macaroni and cheese to the pork chop. As a matter of fact, when I came home, that was the first meal I wanted—stuffed bell peppers, macaroni, pork chop and peas. When I came home from prison! That was my come-home meal right there. When I was gone, that was one of the things I was missing the most, my momma's food. And my business partner, Guillotine, his mom cooks too. She cooks all the wild game: coon and rabbit and deer. She can cook one of your shoes and make it tender. For real.

Eating in prison was horrible. We used to eat in our locker; we called it eating in our box. You can go to the kitchen and get beans—again!—beans, beans, beans, and that deterred me from liking red beans. Red beans used to be one of my favorite dishes, but after eating red beans every day, I don't want to see a red bean again.

I eat horrible. Fast food. But my favorite dish is seafood. I like crab legs and shrimp. Crawfish, I tear them out the frame. If you eat crawfish with me, you'd better be a professional because you won't eat many. Whoever eats the fastest eats the most. And if you're being slow, peeling one shell at a time, I got five-eight-twenty on you right quick. Keep up!

We just did a crawfish boil for Snoop [Dogg]. Oh man, we did some crawfish. He's got like a 33-man production team that he travels with, so we hooked him up. We did a few hundred pounds of crawfish, and they tore it up. Loved it. We seasoned it to perfection.

I'm working on my mixtape, Fish Grease. I'm calling it Fish Grease because it's the prelude to my album, and before you put French fries in the grease, you've got to heat it up. I've got to heat the streets up, and the mixtape will do that for me. The fish is the protein for your body, and that's the music. Analogy—exactly.

We're expecting another baby this December and that's another plate we've got to fill up. She's a great mom. I cook mostly for her. She wants her eggs fried hard and her meats cooked well, and we're straight up with that. She went through a water and lemon phase, so I got good at squeezing lemons. We had to get a lemon budget. I had to get a bottomless sack of lemons every week.

I picked up a lot of cooking tips in prison too. Different little spices and things you can do to kick things up. Like honey, I never would have put no damn honey in my tuna fish. Ever! But man, that shit gives it a twist.

You make a little side dish, we call it a hookup. When you're in prison and you want to eat, and you don't want to go in the kitchen, you just say, 'You want a hookup?' 'Yeah, let's hook something up.' You get your refried beans, and every meal is going to have a ramen soup at the bottom of it. Whether you make a penitentiary lasagna or burritos or whatever it is you're making, some kind of

tuna hookup, barbecue beef hookup, sloppy joe kind of thing. All kinds of concoctions. Six years, I became one of the best hookup persons in there. Was pretty much a chef in there for my comrades.

Some of our meals were expensive, $20-$30. That's a lot of food in prison. As long as you have some refried beans, some beef sticks, you're ready. Get yourself a few soups, and the macaroni and cheese is going down. We have a microwave and a microwave is all we need. That's our heat source and we run with it. You've got to be like Robin Caruso [sic]—you've got to improvise! I became a coffee drinker in prison. The way I am now with it, prison did that. I was more of a sipper, but after that, shit. Like they say, when you're in Rome, do like the Romans. I picked that up, and I never smoked no damn tobacco either, and now I'm chronic. I was a weed smoker. Hickory, chicory, dock.

You've got to come in the kitchen with the right attitude. Don't come in here with your mouth all crooked. That food gonna get awful.

Now I'm going to make the pancakes. I add a little extract, vanilla or almond, whatever you like. Maybe a teaspoon—just an eyeful. One egg, and flour depends on how many you're serving for. Milk to consistency, not too loosey goosey. Salt? Hell no! Get out of my kitchen. Scram! No, we're going sweet. Who wants salty pancakes? Just the thought.

[Pouring coffee into an Obama cup] Bam! Three or four [tablespoons of sugar]. We're going to sweeten his policy up. Come on, chicory. Now, that's a cup of coffee!

Funny story, when I first came home, after the charge I had, I had to send out sex-offender notifications, and people was inviting me to their house, 'Welcome to the neighborhood!' That shit supposed to be like a warning,

Mystikal at New Orleans Jazz & Heritage Festival
Photo by Golden G. Richard, III

## Mystikal's Breakfast

Cook green onion sausage on a George Foreman grill until done. Grill chicken breast strips on there too, squeezing some yellow mustard over it once the surface is cooked, then keep grilling until cooked through. Prepare grits for four people according to directions on package, adding one stick of butter and four slices of yellow American cheese 5 minutes before serving—cover, let melt, stir. "Get yourself a can of Grands Flaky Layers biscuit dough from Wal-Mart, or make biscuits from scratch." Prepare peppered bacon (bacon generously sprinkled with black pepper) in the oven, finishing it off for 1 minute (covered with a paper towel) in the microwave. Make scrambled eggs by mixing four eggs and a splash of milk (and plenty of salt and black pepper) in a bowl; cook in a hot, greased pan. Mystikal calls these "military eggs" because they're cooked hard, and "that's what they used to look like when I was in the Army."

### Pancakes

like, this is a bad man in your neighborhood, time to be leery of him. Shit, I got some invites, people coming to the door.

Any meats, especially chicken, you have to clean it. You soak that shit. We soak our chicken in the sink. When I grew up, I used to wonder why my mama had food just sitting soaking in the sink. 'You've got to wash that food, boy.' Right."

1 cup flour
1 teaspoon baking powder
1 egg
1 cup buttermilk (or milk—then use less)
1 teaspoon extract (vanilla or almond)
½ stick butter, for frying

Stir flour and baking powder together. Mix egg, buttermilk, and extract in a separate bowl. Quickly stir everything together, being careful not to over-mix or let the batter sit too long. Melt about a tablespoon of butter in a frying pan for each pancake. Make pancakes large.

**IN THE KITCHEN WITH**

# Johnette Downing

*"food doesn't have an agenda."*

**BORN**
1962 in Marrero, Louisiana

**NEIGHBORHOOD**
Carrollton

**INSTRUMENTS**
Vocals, guitar

**NOTABLE RECORDING**
"Today is Monday in Louisiana,"
*From the Gumbo Pot,* 1998

**HOLY TRINITY**
Tony's Chachere's Creole Seasoning,
parsley, garlic

**JOHNETTE DOWNING WILL TRY JUST ABOUT ANYTHING, FROM CRAWFISH TO CAMEL:** "I learned to cook from my grandmother who lived in St. Amant, near Gonzales. She was Creole—French, Spanish, and Native American—and she was the best cook. The only thing I didn't learn to cook from her was gumbo because she'd always say, 'Start with a roux.' And I'd say, 'What's a roux?' And she'd say, 'You know what a roux is! Just start with a roux!' But I didn't. She wasn't patient enough; she would just exasperate.

The first time I made a roux, I got the jar of roux. I still use the jar because I really don't know how to make a roux the way you're supposed to do it. I've made it before, just with flour and oil and onions, but it doesn't come out like her roux so I'm not happy. I always stop too soon because I'm afraid I'm going to burn it.

In Louisiana, music and food go hand in hand. I mean, that's what we're all about: music and food. No surprise that my music, since I'm from Louisiana, a lot of my songs have to do with food. I wrote this song called 'Today is Monday in Louisiana.' It's based on a traditional song, but I was looking at the ingredients, all the dishes in the traditional song, and they were Monday roast beef, then chicken and string beans, and I said, 'I have to do this for

Louisiana. We have the best food in the world!' So I did Monday red beans, Tuesday po-boys, Wednesday gumbo, Thursday jambalaya, Friday catfish, Saturday crawfish and Sunday beignets. That song was a really big hit; it's still one of my biggest hits. And because of that song, a lady was in the audience with her son and she came up to me and said, 'Can I illustrate that song and make it into a book?' and that's how the books started. We did *My Aunt Came Back from Louisiane* and *Chef Creole* and both have food in them.

I do about 250 shows a year so I travel a lot, but any time I'm home, I like to cook. I do it as often as possible. I use my *Today is Monday in Louisiana* book when I travel, and I travel internationally and use the book as a cultural bridge. I'll sing my version and then, whatever country I'm in, let's say I'm in Oman, we'll do their version. They might have biryani, shish kebab, or whatever foods they have in their culture, and then we'll talk about the foods we have in common. Food is a great way to reach other cultures. Food doesn't have an agenda.

When I give concerts and workshops in other countries, I'll say 'What do we have in common?' and usually it's rice. Or fish, depending on where it is. But usually rice, so I say, 'See, children? We're really all just rice. We can be brown rice or jasmine rice or saffron rice; long-grain rice or short-grain rice, but really we're just all rice.' Food is non-threatening, non-political, and it's just a nice way to connect the world, I find.

The funny thing about traveling and being from New Orleans is that wherever I go, I'll eat anything. I went to Morocco and I had camel. I'm not sure I want to eat camel again, but I tried it. It was kind of spongy, almost like tofu, and it's a camel color. People like when you'll try. I'm not a picky eater because I live here. We'll try anything and people appreciate that. It's a way of being accepting and open to new ideas and concepts and traditions and new ways of living, different from your own culture. I've learned that. My grandmother always made hogshead cheese and just the idea of it, 'I'm not eating hogshead cheese.' So I never tried it, but the other night my boyfriend and I went to Cochon and they gave us a complimentary piece of hogshead cheese, so I tried it. And it was so good. All this time, I never tried it! I know my grandmother's, it must have been great because people would come over when they found out she was cooking. I missed the opportunity to try hers."

## Sausage Mambo

Johnette enjoys this dish by itself, but you could easily serve it over rice or pasta. Actually, this recipe constitutes half of Johnette's jambalaya recipe as well. The other half is Zatarain's jambalaya mix. "Like they say, don't fix what ain't broke. It works and it's great. Just add an extra handful of plain rice."

1 link Polska kielbasa sausage (Hillshire Farm)
2 tablespoons olive oil
2 tablespoons Worcestershire sauce
1 tablespoon dried parsley
1 teaspoon Tony Chachere's Creole Seasoning
1 yellow onion, diced
5 cloves garlic, chopped
1 yellow bell pepper, diced
1 orange bell pepper, diced

Sausage Mambo

Johnette Downing performs for 335 kids at
the Jazz National Historical Park

1 red bell pepper, diced
½ tub sliced mushrooms

Slice sausage into doubloons. Heat oil and Worcestershire
sauce in a skillet. Sauté sausage until deep red in color,
adding parsley and Tony Chachere's. Add onion and
garlic. When onion becomes translucent, add bell peppers
and mushrooms. Sauté until vegetables are tender.

## IN THE KITCHEN WITH

# Marcia Ball

"Mostly it was rice; we were in rice country."

**BORN**
1949 in Orange, Texas

**NEIGHBORHOOD**
Zilker, Austin, TX

**INSTRUMENTS**
Piano

**NOTABLE RECORDING**
"That's Enough of That Stuff,"
*Live! Down the Road*, 2005

**HOLY TRINITY**
Garlic, garlic, garlic

**MARCIA BALL HAS SPENT ENOUGH TIME TRAVELING THE I-10 CORRIDOR TO PARSE OUT THE REGIONAL DIFFERENCES IN LOUISIANA COOKING:** "I get to cook about half the time. We play about 125 gigs a year, so I'm only here about half the time. I'm also blessed with a husband who cooks and really, he's the foodie in the family; the more adventurous, the more interesting cook. He'll open a cookbook and do something creative. I, on the other hand, will come in and make a gumbo or an étouffée or something out of my head, the same old stuff. I love to cook smothered pork chops or round steak. I don't use tomato; I don't put tomato in almost anything. I finally learned to eat spaghetti and pizza, but when I was a kid I didn't like anything that had tomato gravy on it.

I grew up in Vinton, Louisiana. It's interesting, even then I could recognize the different styles of Louisiana cooking. The brown gravies were different from the way my grandmother in New Orleans cooked. New Orleans seemed to have more of what you call the holy trinity, more aware of the bell pepper and the celery and the onion. Whereas down in Vinton or Lafayette—my other grandmother was from Lafayette—you just really got a brown gravy that was just brown. With onion, mainly. Didn't use much of the bell pepper or the celery. I'm not a big celery fan, either. This is my guilty secret; I like raw celery, but I don't like celery in food. I'm not crazy about the texture so I just leave it out. But garlic, green onions, and parsley, I love all that stuff, so I do that. Often, I use the white part of the green onion when I put in the rest of the onion, and then I put the green onion [tops] on top, at the end. I will never forget the first time I ate at Chez Helene in New Orleans and that wonderful gumbo with a sprinkle of fresh green onion on top, across it, it was just like art, beautiful. That was the first time I became aware of the art of the presentation. That was 25 years ago.

Daddy's favorite meal was round steak cooked the same way as my mother's smothered pork chops but without the sugar, and served with rice and gravy and cream-style corn. My favorite meal was the smothered pork chops with mashed potatoes and canned sweet peas with a little bit of bacon grease and onion. Mostly it was rice; mashed potatoes would be like a special treat because we were in rice country.

My mother grew up near Thibodaux, in Labadieville, and that's something else. In Vinton, we didn't eat a lot of crawfish. Crawfish was something we ate when we went down to Thibodaux to visit my aunts. I remember going to New Orleans for Easter and seeing all the cars stopped along Airline Highway, the whole road from Baton Rouge to New Orleans, and people were down there crawfishing by the side of the road where the bayous crossed.

Me sticking to Louisiana cooking probably means that I'm lazy, and also that I married a guy who cooks. It used to be my trick—buy whatever I thought I wanted for supper and come in and flop it on the counter and start rattling pots and pans. Gordon would come in and take over and I would make a salad. He'll reduce sauces and he cooks with wine, braises lamb shanks. Right now, I'm exploring some Asian food. I made my first coconut milk soup. And for years, for my kids, the Thai beef salad. I use sirloin and cut it across the grain, real thin, and flash it in the pan, real rare, and do a bed of lettuce and tomato and thin slices of red and green bell pepper and onion, thin slivers, and some peanuts and a little bit of fish sauce and lots and lots of lime juice and green onion tops and mint and basil all tossed in there. That's what my son wanted for his birthday dinner last August. He was 33. When I turned 33, a layer of insecurity and uncertainty fell away that made me more comfortable in my skin."

## Smothered Pork Chops

The brown gravy in this recipe relies on roux of a different kind—instead of flour, Marcia Ball stirs sugar into the hot oil.

8 thin-cut pork chops
Salt
Black pepper
¼ cup vegetable oil
2 tablespoons sugar
1 yellow onion, sliced
2 cloves garlic, sliced
1 tablespoon flour

Season pork chops with salt and pepper. Heat oil in a heavy pot, cast-iron, or Magnalite Dutch oven. Add sugar and let it caramelize; "it burns pretty much." Add pork

Smothered Pork Chops

Marcia Ball, with Don Bennett on bass,
at the Crescent City Blues & BBQ Festival

chops and "flop 'em around." When thoroughly smeared, add onion and garlic. Fry for a few minutes. Add ½ cup water to start the gravy. Dissolve flour in another ½ cup water and add to pot. Cover and simmer over low heat for at least 30 minutes, adding more water if necessary. You want a rich—not soupy—gravy.

## IN THE KITCHEN WITH

# Julia LaShae

**SINGER JULIA LASHAE DOESN'T MESS WITH MOLE:** "My family is from south Texas and my grandfather got a job with Gulf Oil. They had oil camps down in the countries where they had their oil fields, and my grandparents moved down to Venezuela. My father actually spent most of his childhood there. My grandmother started to learn all these Venezuelan recipes and got really good at them. They came back when my father was in college. After my father got married and they had all of us, my grandmother would always make these Venezuelan recipes. Every Saturday, she'd make chilaquiles and chicken mole. She'd make her version of tacos, which were more like flautas—rolled and fried. She'd make guacamole, which is my favorite food, always has been. My mom said that my little sister and I would sit at the table with one tortilla chip, one big Frito, and we would sit there and lick the guacamole off the chip. We didn't know you were supposed to eat the chip. Being born in the southern part of Texas, we were around Tex-Mex all the time, but you could tell that there was a difference between what we ate at my grandmother's house and what you ate when you went to the Tex-Mex restaurants in town.

I should make mole more often. I make it more for special occasions these days. I have Celiac disease, so everything has to be glu-

**BORN**
1969 in Austin, Texas

**NEIGHBORHOOD**
Mid-City

**INSTRUMENTS**
Vocals

**NOTABLE RECORDING**
"How High the Moon,"
*Introducing... Julia LaShae*, 2002

**HOLY TRINITY**
Masa harina, cumin, buffalo

ten-free. Almost everything that my grandmother made from Venezuela is corn-based, and corn doesn't have gluten in it, so I should make it more often than I do. I tend to make a lot of grilled food, and veggies, but when I have time—I'll show you, you actually have to let the mole simmer for an hour or two, so it's not something to make when you're really hungry and need to eat immediately.

My grandmother always served corn tortillas with butter and salt; that was what we would eat for bread. No Bunny bread. Maybe that's why I didn't get diagnosed with Celiac disease until I got older, when I started to eat more whole-grain wheat bread, trying to be healthy, but I just got sick, really sick.

With mole, you want to put all of your flavors in with the fat first, and get all of that melded together and then you add your tomato juice and your broth. You need to use a big stew pot. We always cooked big in our family. In our family, we have five kids, and my grandmother was one of nine, so we're used to making really large amounts.

When my grandmother was getting older, all of us wanted copies of her recipes, this amazing Venezuelan food that we didn't have access to any other way. We asked her, but she did all of them in her head. She didn't have anything written down, and she couldn't tell you.

So for about a week, my older sister followed her and wrote down everything, how she did it. She couldn't even tell you the measurements. She'd just pour it in her hand and throw it in there, so my sister measured everything, a teaspoon, a tablespoon. This is my older sister's handwriting.

My grandmother was probably in her late forties when she came back to the States. When my sister went over to her house and followed her, she was close to 80. She had been back for over 30 years and she was still cooking Venezuelan food almost every Saturday. Every now and then, she'd do a pot roast or something, but it was almost always chilaquiles in a casserole style, or chicken mole or the tacos or enchiladas. Every now and then she'd make tamales for us. It was hearty winter food, comfort food. She still made it like she was still there.

I cook mole for Rob, my boyfriend. And when my family gets together, I usually make the chicken enchiladas and we had that instead of turkey at Thanksgiving.

With the enchiladas recipe, we've made little adjustments along the way, added different ingredients. Sometimes, we make it with black beans while my grandmother only used pinto beans. We're not competitive about food, my siblings and I. It's more that we tend to take the recipes and, 'Hey, I tried this,' and get tips from each other, how to make it better, but I don't think it's possible to improve on grandma's recipes. We try different things, but me, I go back to her recipes the way she did them because they taste the best and that's how I remember it. I've tried her guacamole recipe with cooked onions instead of the raw, and that's really good. But the mole recipe I don't mess with."

## Grandma Bula's Mole

"I tend to like a thinner sauce because I like it to really soak into the meat and the rice." Serve this sauce warm over shredded chicken or pork (or anything, really).

6 tablespoons (mild) chili powder
2 tablespoons sugar

Grandma Bula's Mole

Julia LaShae at the Mystick Den
Photo by Rob Hebert

1 tablespoon salt
1 tablespoon cocoa
½ teaspoon cinnamon
4 tablespoons lard, bacon drippings, or chicken fat
2 tablespoons creamy peanut butter
1 (6-ounce) can tomato paste
3 cups tomato juice
1½ quarts chicken broth
4 tablespoons corn starch

Mix dry spices. Heat lard in heavy pot or Dutch oven. Fry spices in fat for 1 minute. Stir as not to burn. Add pea-nut butter and cook slowly about 3 minutes. Add tomato paste and juice. Dissolve cornstarch in 1 cup of broth, then add this with remaining broth. Cover and simmer for at least 1 hour.

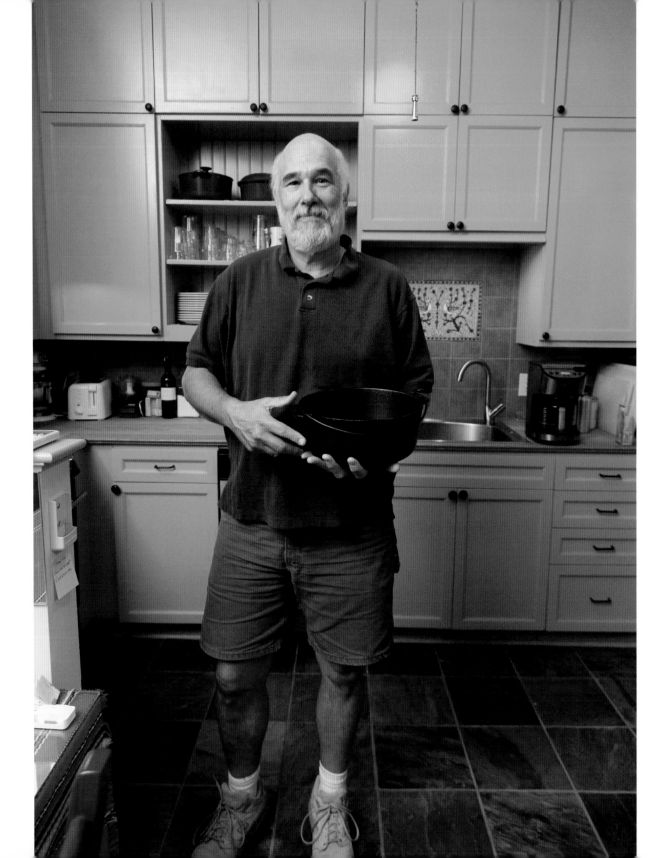

**IN THE KITCHEN WITH**

# David Doucet

**GUITARIST DAVID DOUCET COOKS IN HIS MOTHER'S AND GRANDMOTHER'S POTS:** "We had a disagreement. We had a difference of views because when I was a kid, my grandmother used to make a dish she called crab stew, but it wasn't written down. I have no idea how you make that. And in Lafayette, there was this [cookbook] that came out called *Talk About Good*. One of the crawfish recipes we cooked came from that. Paul Prudhomme's first book, *Louisiana Cooking*, for me, that's the book. But he doesn't make a crab stew either, although his crawfish étouffée is very close to a stew because his étouffée is not really an étouffée, because you make étouffée out of butter. We adapted that. Then DeDe pulls out *Talk About Good*, which is almost illegible because it's full of crab juice and crawfish guts. My recipe is a combination of three or four different things, which kind of makes it my own.

I make my roux fast. My mother used to be a two-beer rouxer. That takes too long; about 30 minutes. Fast is the way to go—Prudhomme. But you have to be careful.

Use your grandmother's pots if you can. I wanted to have her pots because I wanted to cook! And they don't make them like this anymore. My grandmother was Lucille LeBlanc, and she married a LeBlanc, so she was L.L.L. on all her stuff.

**"How's my butter doing? Doing real good."**

**BORN**
1957 in Lafayette, Louisiana

**NEIGHBORHOOD**
Touro

**INSTRUMENTS**
Guitar, ukulele, Acadian accordion

**NOTABLE RECORDING**
"L'ouragon (The Hurricane)," BeauSoleil, *Our New Orleans: A Benefit Album*, Various Artists, 2005

**HOLY TRINITY**
Garlic, onion, celery

This is a three-pot dish. This is not what you do in Cajun land. This is all Prudhomme and Frank [Brigtsen]. We use stock; Cajuns use water. Prudhomme tells you how to basically use restaurant techniques in your home kitchen, and you can't change anything. How many times do you think he cooked that stuff in order to write it like that? He's a nut in the kitchen, but if you follow him, it never scorches, it never sticks; it always does what it's supposed to do.

We travel all over America, and in our rider for Beau-Soleil, it says, 'Under no circumstances can you feed the band Cajun food.' Because invariably, you go somewhere, 'I made Prudhomme's gumbo,' and you look at it and it's beige because they don't do it right. Pineapple in the gumbo—that was Atlanta, Georgia. They just keep adding shit. Fusion, baby. Occasionally you run into someone who can actually do it. There was one guy in Maine, and a couple in Tennessee. It's dangerous to get invited to someone's house. Here we are, seven Cajuns walking around the planet—'I'm going to make you a Cajun breakfast!' Sometimes we have no choice.

We have about 80 gigs a year and you need a day to get there, so we're traveling about half the year. We know every ethnic restaurant in America. We thought about doing a guidebook, but we didn't want to tell anybody where we eat (or people might show up with Cajun food). We eat Mexican food, Lebanese food, Thai food. Coffee, traveling as much as we do, that's the other thing. I've always brought a coffee pot and coffee on the road.

Some traveling salesman came through in the '40s or '50s and sold us this machine. It was handheld; you put a potato on it and turn and it'd make potato chips. It was almost hand-made, and I love potatoes. That was a very good thing. We had some property and this guy there farming, and he'd always bring a crate of potatoes every year, that was part of his rent. He'd bring the potatoes, which my dad would use for crawfish boils or potato chips. I didn't get this big not eating them, I'll tell you that.

[My brother] Michael and I argue about how to make gumbo. I make the Paul Prudhomme gumbo and if you follow his recipe, including frying the chicken, it's an all-day affair. With Cajun gumbo, you boil everything in one pot. With Paul Prudhomme, you use lots of pots.

Here's another pot to clean. This is where it gets gross, where you get your flavor. It's an obscene amount of butter. How's my butter doing? Doing real good. Crab and butter go great together. It's kind of a waste to use jumbo lump, but it's good. You could put another stick of butter in here, you could. But I don't know if it needs it."

# Crab Stew

### Seafood stock (makes 4 cups)

2 quarts cold water
1 onion, unpeeled and quartered
1 head garlic, unpeeled and cut
1 carrot
1 rib celery
1 teaspoon black peppercorns
1-2 pounds of gumbo crabs

### Roux

7 tablespoons vegetable oil
¾ cup flour

### Chopped vegetables

½ cup finely chopped onion
¼ cup finely chopped celery
¼ cup finely chopped green bell pepper
1 garlic clove, finely chopped

### Seasoning mix

2 teaspoons salt
1–2 teaspoons cayenne
1 teaspoon white pepper
1 teaspoon black pepper
1 teaspoon dried sweet basil
½ teaspoon thyme leaves

### Finishing touches

1 stick butter
½ cup finely chopped green onions
1 pound crabmeat (jumbo lump)

David Doucet at Chickie Wah Wah with Washboard Chaz

Make stock by simmering all ingredients together for 25 minutes. Strain, and set aside.

In a cast-iron Dutch oven, heat oil to nearly smoking, then whisk in flour. Simmer and stir constantly until roux is dark red-brown. Remove from heat and stir in chopped vegetables and 1 tablespoon seasoning mix. Turn heat to medium/low and continue to stir until vegetables soften and shine, 5-10 minutes.

In a 2-quart saucepan, bring 2 cups stock to a boil. Gradually add roux mixture until dissolved. Reduce heat and cook for 2 or 3 minutes, until the flour taste is gone, stir-ring constantly. In a 4-quart saucepan, melt butter. Stir in crabmeat and green onion. Add roux mixture, remaining stock, crab bodies, and remaining seasoning mix. Simmer for 10 minutes. Serve in bowls over hot rice, accompanied by French bread and beer.

# IN THE KITCHEN WITH

## Theresa Andersson

**THERESA ANDERSSON FELL FAR FROM THE TREE:** "I didn't cook much when I lived in Sweden. I was 18 when I moved here, and that was basically when I started my own home. We planted our lemon tree five years ago. I grew up on a farm so I love plants. I didn't know this before I moved here; I love being in the garden. Right now it's in pretty good shape, but when we travel it grows wild. This summer, we were gone for three months, so now we mainly have a lot of mint and basil out there. I make a lot of pesto.

I always wanted to pick an orange off a tree; I'd never done that. But they didn't have any orange trees the day we went to the store, and we saw lemon trees, so now I pick lemons instead of oranges. It's a Meyer lemon and it started carrying fruit after just one year. Only a couple of lemons, but then it exploded. The bees and the monarch butterflies love it, which is good. They're friendly. You just have to watch where you put your hands and not inhale a bee accidentally. There must be 200 or 300 lemons on here. It's intense.

In the past I've used lemons for juicing. I make fresh juices with kale, carrots, apples, lemons, and you can put the whole thing in the juicer, with the rind and everything. I also make lemonade. In our English lessons in Sweden, they were talking about lemonade a

*"I've been a vegetarian since I was five years old."*

**BORN**
1971 in Gotland, Sweden

**NEIGHBORHOOD**
Algiers Point

**INSTRUMENTS**
Vocals, violin, guitar, loop pedal, drums

**NOTABLE RECORDING**
"Birds Fly Away,"
*Hummingbird, Go!*, 2008

**HOLY TRINITY**
Lemon, Celtic sea salt, olive oil

lot. I was maybe nine. I'd never had it, but I pictured it as being sparkly and tangy. It took 10 years before I tasted some, but it was a dream come true. No one knew how to make lemonade back home. My mom tried to squeeze some oranges one time and put sugar in it.

This year, I'm trying something new—preserved lemons with salt and olive oil. You can use them for grilled fish, stews, or in couscous. They're salty and tangy, like some weird olive. I was blown away when I first tasted it last year. There's a little cafe here in the Point called Tout De Suite, and that's where I tried it. First I was like 'Erh, I don't know about that.' And then I was like, 'Give me more! I want more!' Maybe I'll get adventurous with some ice cream and put little pieces in there. Salty and sweet is a good combination.

When I get off the road, I don't like driving around too much. I like staying at home because I do enough car time. After *Hummingbird, Go!* I was on the road pretty much straight. When I'm home, I cook everyday. We cook a lot, and we compost everything from the kitchen. We have worm bins with African red wigglers. They're moody. If it's too cold, you have to bring them inside. You have to be able to take care of them. We've had times when they've died, which is very sad, but we have friends who come over and feed them when we're out of town.

If you buy plants from Lowe's or Home Depot and something dies and you have your receipt and the container it came in, you can bring it back. I bought my lemon tree at Home Depot. Didn't have to bring it back, though. I try to have stuff in the garden that takes care of itself, things that bloom when I'm usually home. The mums are wonderful because they come back and bloom three times.

I've been a vegetarian since I was five years old. I just started refusing the meat and the fish and the chicken— all that. I tried chicken for a while and quickly stopped. But fish I've been eating since I came here.

I have a couple of quick soup recipes. Carrot soup I learned from my mom. We used to grow carrots on the farm. It's quick to make and absolutely delicious. You take five carrots and peel them and coarsely grate them. Sauté them with a couple of cloves of crushed garlic in two to three tablespoons of olive oil. Then you pour 10 cups of water on them, so they're swimming, and add three tablespoons of Better Than Bouillon and a shake of ground white pepper. Bring it to a boil and simmer for 10 minutes—done!

[Grating carrots] This will make good worm food. The worms don't like citrus and they don't like onion, but they're crazy about this.

I can't stand this house in December, honestly. There is no insulation. We've been working on all the little leaky spots, but there are so many more and the floors are cold. Last year we had to check into a hotel for a couple of those cold days because it was just unbearable."

## Preserved Meyer Lemons

12 large Meyer lemons
1 cup coarse kosher salt
4 pint-size canning jars
¼ cup (or more) olive oil

Wash whole lemons. Boil 6 lemons in plenty of water for 5 minutes, remove from water and let cool. Boil glass jars

Meyer lemon tree in Theresa Andersson's backyard

Theresa Andersson at Le Petit Theatre
Photo by Erica Folse

for 15 minutes; soak lids in hot water for 10 minutes; remove jars and lids from water and let dry. Cut lemons into eighths, removing seeds and center white membrane. Coat each piece with salt and pack tightly into jars. Juice remaining 6 lemons and pour juice over salted lemon pieces in jars to cover. Screw on lids. Let sit in room temperature for 5 days, shaking jars once a day. Pour olive oil on top. Refrigerate. Use within a year.

**IN THE KITCHEN WITH**

## Irma Thomas

"You know you're home when you've got a pot of beans cooking. "

**BORN**
1941 in Ponchatoula, Louisiana

**NEIGHBORHOOD**
New Orleans East

**INSTRUMENTS**
Vocals

**NOTABLE RECORDING**
"Wish Someone Would Care,"
*Wish Someone Would Care*, 1964

**HOLY TRINITY**
Onion, bell pepper, celery

IRMA THOMAS MAY LIKE VEGETABLES, BUT SHE KNOWS WHAT'S IMPORTANT IN MACARONI AND CHEESE: "I was raised in Greensburg, Louisiana, for most of my young childhood. My father took me to live with his mother—I must have been about five years old—but the same year she passed away, so I went to live with her sister with six kids. In the country, the oldest kid in the family was the designated cook, who was my cousin, Lil' Berta. Usually, your meals were fresh out of the fields. It was either greens or beans, whatever was in season at that time, and our meats were smokehouse meats, either ham or some beef or something they had in storage. We didn't eat a lot of meat that I can remember. Mostly vegetables. Meat was maybe once or twice a week.

I don't remember being sick as a growing kid. Once a month, you got your annual dose of castor oil. I hated oranges for a long time because they gave you an orange to suck on after you'd taken the castor oil. So for a long time, I would not eat an orange. And then when my kids were growing up, I did them the same thing.

I started cooking as a kid. Nine years old, my father put me on a Coke crate. We used them for stools, and my father put the crate to the stove. That's where I stood and learned how to cook. He started me off with frying eggs and bacon and cooking grits, and from there I graduated to cooking beans, and from there to greens, and from then I'd cook anything that I want. My mom was not the big cook in the house. I was.

My favorite recipes, you don't have to cook. I'm a salad person. It can be all vegetables, just the plain, garden variety of lettuces. I'm not too big on iceberg lettuce, but I do like the young lettuce leaves. Mix them up, throw some cucumbers and carrots in there, and I'm good to go. When I do cook, I bake chickens. I like that.

And I love cobblers, that's why I'm always on a diet. Peach cobbler, blackberry cobbler. For the pastry, I use Bisquick. You can only do so much damage with Bisquick. I'm not going to lie to you and tell you I'm doing it from scratch. I've even used canned buttermilk biscuits as a quick fix. You just cut them up in little pieces and drop them in the cobbler and bake it. Smush 'em a little bit, so they'll think you've worked a lot.

As far as my meals, I lean more toward the salads and the vegetable dishes. I do love lasagna and I am crazy about the eggplant parmesan. Oh God, I love that stuff. So I don't know why I'm so fat, because all the foods I love are not fattening. I think it's got a lot to do with my schedule, and I don't get to eat on a regular basis like I should. But when we have a break, I fix a meal. Usually I put a pot of red beans on, something that doesn't require a lot of attention. And it definitely soothes my husband to smell the beans cooking in the house. You know you're home when you've got a pot of beans cooking.

My husband, Emile, is a country boy. He loves his country meals; he's a rice and gravy man, so he gets his rice and gravy. Brown gravies, red gravies. He likes meatballs and spaghetti, smothered pork chops. He likes his smothered chicken, take a hen and smother it. Smothered turkey necks, I do those, too. I fix up a big pan of smothered turkey necks and make some macaroni and cheese.

In the country, you tend to use more gravies and fillers to stretch things because most of the country families were large, so they'd fix a meal that would spread over a large family. Gravies, something filling. Beans is a dominant factor there, greens is a dominant factor. I'll never forget—I guess it was my first year of marriage with my husband—I caught myself fixing him a really neat city meal; I stuffed some pork chops with apple dressing and I made some vegetables on the side and a salad. When he sat down at the table, he asked me, 'Where was the rice and gravy?' And I have not stuffed pork chops since. It's been 30 years."

## Macaroni and Cheese

When Irma Thomas is left with an extra cheese tray after a party, she makes macaroni and cheese. Or rather, cheese and macaroni. "The macaroni is a plus, 'cause the cheese is what you're dealing with."

1 pound uncooked elbow macaroni
2 tablespoons butter
1 pound cheese, cut into small cubes (a mix of pepper jack, gouda, sharp and mild cheddar, colby jack)
1 large cooking spoon granulated sugar (roughly ¼ cup)
3 eggs, beaten
1 cup milk
Vegetable oil spray

Macaroni and Cheese

Irma Thomas at New Orleans Jazz & Heritage Festival
Photo by Kim Welsh

Cook macaroni according to directions on the box, until almost done. Drain and butter pasta. Add cheese, sugar, eggs, and milk. Stir. Spray a lasagna pan or other deep dish with vegetable oil. Dump in the macaroni and cheese mix. Bake in the oven at 350 degrees for 30-45 minutes.

# IN THE KITCHEN WITH

## James Westfall

**VIBRAPHONIST JAMES WESTFALL HAS HIS OWN THREE-SECOND RULE:** "Originally from Houston, I basically learned to make smoked brisket from everyone in the family. Most of my family comes from cattle barons; there's always a bunch of beef around. It's kind of like here, where everyone knows how to make red beans and rice. In Texas, everyone knows how to smoke barbecue.

I make smoked brisket maybe twice a month. It's an all-day thing. Kind of like making red beans, you let it go and go do other things, go to the store and come back, go do whatever and come back, make sure the fire is still set. I like to keep the temperature between 150 and 200. The heat and the smoke come from the offset firebox and go through here, through the barrel. There are electric smokers that'll keep the set temperature with propane, but this is using charcoal and wood, so you always have to adjust. If it gets too hot you have to close the vents a little bit, or if it gets too low, open the vents and add some coals. Propane will keep the temperature at a steady 250, which is too hot to smoke brisket. It'll come out dry. With charcoal, you have to check it often, but you get a lower heat and it's more traditional. It's always the propane versus the charcoal debate, but charcoal is usually the way to go. You'll get a lot of flack

**BORN**
1981 in Houston, Texas

**NEIGHBORHOOD**
Upper Ninth Ward

**INSTRUMENTS**
Vibraphone, piano, keytar, vocals

**NOTABLE RECORDING**
"About a Girl (Kurt Cobain),"
*Capitol Diner Vol. 1*, The Wee Trio, 2008

**HOLY TRINITY**
Hickory wood, salt, pepper

if you don't cook over charcoal in Texas. Use propane and it's considered being lazy. It's like eating Blue Runner's red beans instead of making them yourself.

I use hickory wood because I like the flavor. You can buy it at the grocery store in packs; sometimes you can find them at gas stations. Wherever they sell charcoal, they'll sell the wood. It comes in little chips and you soak the chips in water for 30 minutes and they'll add the flavor and the smoke.

The meat shrinks when you cook it. We usually get a big cut, 10 to 12 pounds, but sometime you don't want to be out here for 12 hours or more. Today we got a smaller cut. With a seven-pound cut, I can be out here for about eight hours. You smoke it for about an hour or more per pound. You don't want the butcher to cut all the fat off because you want to put the fat on the topside, about three-quarters of an inch. Brisket is a tough cut of meat, and you have to slow-cook it. Knowing when it's done is a little bit of a guess, a bit like seeing and knowing. Some people say you should be able to put a fork in it and lift it up, but you don't want to do that. After the brisket is cooked you want to let it sit for about 30 minutes to an hour, just on a plate. If you cut it right away, all the juices are going to come out and it's going to get dry. After it sits you can trim the fat off.

When you buy the cut, you want it to make a semi-circle when you pick it up in the middle, kind of let it drape over your hand. Then you know there's enough fat inside. If it stays kind of straight, it's going to be tough and chewy.

I got this pit from Jesse McBride. It was his neighbor's and his neighbor left it and Jesse was the last one to move out of his building. He called me and his friend had a truck. It is really heavy. It takes two people just to roll it.

Once we took this to Frenchmen and tailgated our gig. We set it up in front of the Blue Nile, right on a truck. It turned out to be a good leverage tool to get people to gigs, giving them free food. It was a good crowd that night. People were trying to give us money. 'Just buy a ticket. Go inside.'

To keep the meat from drying out, I put a pan of water underneath the meat. It catches the juices and keeps the pit nice and moist. I come out to check the fire about once an hour, add coals or open it up a little bit, add more wood chips; I'll put a couple of handfuls.

I use about three bags of wood chips [100 cubic-inches each]. Coals, I use the three-second rule. If you can put your hand in there for more than three seconds, it's not hot enough. If I see the temperature going down to 150, I throw two to three handfuls of coals in.

When the meat is done, I'll slice it against the grain into half-inch strips. Actually, I'll probably get full by cutting it and eating while I cut it, just standing here. I eat it straight, or on a sandwich, but it's usually more meat than bread. I usually don't make a sauce. I only made a sauce once.

If I'm going to smoke, I'll stick to brisket because brisket is my favorite. I guess I'm just not a pork fan. I do ribs, beef ribs, but then we'll grill, use the smoker as a grill.

For brisket you have to use a dry rub, as opposed to a marinade. A dry rub keeps all the juices inside the meat. About a quarter cup of Bubba's Barbecue Rub for Brisket; I bought this in San Antonio. It's got chili powder, paprika, garlic salt, onion powder, all the basic stuff. I put it all over the meat the day before, cover it with plastic and let it sit in the fridge overnight. Rub it, refrigerate it.

[Shouting to wife in adjacent room:] Can I put something on the record? On whose gumbo is better? Can I go on the record?

Wife: Yes.

Well, she likes my gumbo better than her mom's, and my cooking better than her mom's cooking."

## Smoked Brisket

James Westfall has revised his recipe many times. This is his most recent version.

Buy a 9-pound brisket that is soft enough to drape over your forearm (in the shape of the letter C) two days before you plan to eat it. Wash in cold water and pat dry with paper towels. Rub with a mixture of 90 percent black pepper and 10 percent salt, plus a few dashes of cayenne pepper. Use as much rub as will stick. Wrap in plastic foil and let the brisket rest overnight in the fridge.

Get your smoker (with an offset fire box) going. Smoke at 350 degrees. Too hot? Close vents. Too cold? Add more charcoal and hickory wood into the firebox. Put a metal pan of water at the bottom of the smoker to keep the meat moist. After lighting coals and hickory wood, wait 30 minutes for them to turn gray before placing the brisket in the smoker. (Remove plastic wrap first, of course.) Place the thickest part of the meat closest to the fire, and the fat side down. Check smoker after 2 hours to make sure the internal temperature of the meat is 170 degrees. When the internal temperature reaches 170 degrees, take the brisket out of the smoker and wrap in tin foil with the fat side up. Then put the meat back in the smoker, and cook for another 2 hours. Open smoker as little as possible. "When you're looking, you're not cooking." Place brisket inside a dry cooler ("hot box") for 1 hour before slicing (against the grain).

James Westfall at Irvin Mayfield's Jazz Playhouse at the Royal Sonesta Hotel, with Barry Stephenson on bass

**IN THE KITCHEN WITH**

# Seguenon Kone

IVORY COAST PERCUSSIONIST SEGUENON KONE HAS A
TRICK FOR MAKING FOOD SPICY: *"Chez nous*, the mothers have
to teach their children how to cook. The parents work in the fields
and plant corn, peanuts, yams, and other crops. And when the
plants start to grow, the children have to guard the crops, because
birds and monkeys and squirrels love to eat young plants, and there
might be nothing left to harvest. So all the children work. There
is one field for corn, one field for peanuts, one field for yams, one
field for rice, and one field for yuca. The parents work together as
a team. 'Today you work in my field, tomorrow I work in yours.' So
the parents tour around and tend to the earth, plant and harvest
while the children work together in other fields.

The women in Africa suffer. They work with the men in the fields
and then the women walk all the way back to the village carrying
wood and food, while the men are already gone by bike. Once back
in the village, the women cook. As soon as she arrives, she has to
prepare the evening's meal. While all of this is going on, the man
sits and does nothing, touches nothing. He doesn't have the right
to go into the kitchen; it would be disrespectful. Also, the woman
boils water for the husband's shower. She carries it to the shower,

*"Some people actually won't
eat food that isn't spicy. "*

**BORN**
1962 in Gbon, Ivory Coast

**NEIGHBORHOOD**
Bywater

**INSTRUMENTS**
Djembe, dunun, balafon, vocals

**NOTABLE RECORDING**
"St. James Infirmary Blues,"
*Seguenon Presents Ensemble Fatien*,
Ensemble Fatien, 2010

**HOLY TRINITY**
Bouillon cubes, habañero, tomato

calls her husband, 'Your water is ready,' and when he's done showering, he leaves the bucket for his wife to bring back to the kitchen. She washes everything; she does the dishes, she washes the kids, she cleans the house, and she cooks. The men just eat. That's it. So the woman in Africa needs help! My mother loved to cook, but it was also an obligation.

Today, we are going to cook oxtail, and oxtail takes a long time to cook. When my mother cooked oxtail, the children went far, far away to play. When she cooked chicken, we stayed close by, because chicken cooks fast. You can choose your meat depending on how much time you have.

I never measure my rice; I never measure the water. When you make rice for a lot of people, you don't have time to measure. You just know. If you feel that it's a bit heavy when you stir the rice, you know it's good. If the spoon goes fast, you know you have too much water.

When we cut our okra, we don't throw away the tops. We dry them, and then we smash them in a mortar and sift them. You get like flour and grains. The grains, we call it *djumblé*, and we use it to make another type of gravy. It's my favorite.

In Africa, we prepare a lot of starches. Fufu made with yuca, fufu made with yam, fufu made with plantain. You cook everything for a long time, so you don't have to chop everything so fine. The vegetables fall apart, and if they don't, you mash them. You don't see the individual vegetables in the gravy. If you do, the gravy is not cooked right. If I go to an African restaurant here and see pieces of onion in the sauce, I know the sauce wasn't ready. *Ce n'est pas normal.* I don't go back there.

In Africa, food can be very spicy. Some people actually won't eat food that isn't spicy. I like spicy food so I cook with a lot of hot peppers. I add them whole; this is the trick. When the peppers are cooked, you crush them, but you don't have to crush all of them. I will put six whole jalapeños in here, and if you want a very spicy stew, you crush all of them. But today, I will crush three and leave the other three whole. When I cook for people who don't like spicy food, I don't crush any peppers. If you want it spicy, you serve yourself a pepper and crush it in your bowl."

## Okra Eggplant Stew with Oxtail

The vegetables are cooked for hours until they disintegrate—so don't bother chopping them too fine. Adding the jalapeños whole is a great way to add flavor but almost no heat.

5 pounds oxtail (in pieces about 2 inches thick)
2 pounds okra
1 eggplant
1 yellow onion, chopped
1 bunch green onions, chopped
1 tomato, quartered
3 Maggi beef bouillon cubes
2 tablespoons tomato paste
½ pound whole jalapeño peppers (tops snapped off)
Salt (optional)

Place oxtail meat in a large pot, adding water to cover. While you wait for this to boil, slice okra, discarding tops. Cut off top from eggplant and cut into 8 or 12 huge chunks. Add okra and eggplant to meat. Add yellow

Okra Eggplant Stew with Oxtail

Seguenon Kone at the Apple Barrel

and green onion and tomato to meat. Also, add bouillon cubes and tomato paste. If there is still room in the pot, add jalapeños now. Otherwise wait for vegetables to cook down. Simmer for about 2 hours, stirring carefully from time to time. When meat is soft, remove eggplant and jalapeños. Mash eggplant with a fork; add it back. Mash as many jalapeños as you like, adding them back to the pot as well. (You might want to mash only one jalapeño to start and leave the rest whole. Kone mashes about four, because he likes his food H.O.T.)

## IN THE KITCHEN WITH

# Andrew Duhon

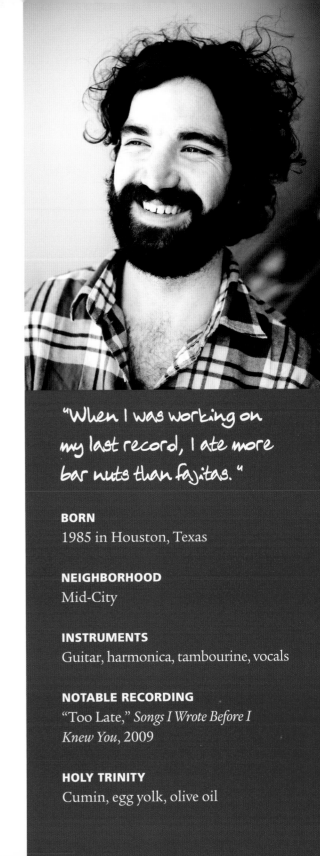

"When I was working on my last record, I ate more bar nuts than fajitas."

**BORN**
1985 in Houston, Texas

**NEIGHBORHOOD**
Mid-City

**INSTRUMENTS**
Guitar, harmonica, tambourine, vocals

**NOTABLE RECORDING**
"Too Late," *Songs I Wrote Before I Knew You*, 2009

**HOLY TRINITY**
Cumin, egg yolk, olive oil

**THE SINGER-SONGWRITER HAS A HEART OF HABANERO:** "This is definitely one of my favorite dishes. I guess I could trace the whole thing back to when my dad and I used to make fajitas. My dad used some store-bought marinade, really close to a salad dressing, and when you'd cook it, it'd reduce to almost a paste and it'd latch on to the beef, or the chicken strips. But you'd have to cook it so long the meat got tough, so I switched to the way I'm cooking it now. I use thighs, or cut the breast into tenderloins, throwing that on the grill to get the nice charred, smoky thing going on, and then cut it into bite-sized pieces.

The other reason I like making fajitas and tacos is that it welcomes that southern tendency, in my mind, to pile on hot things until you can't take it anymore. Jalapeños, peppers, hot sauce, and cayenne all go great with tacos. I almost like to hurt myself with hot sauce sometimes. It becomes culinary masochism if you're not careful.

My parents went to Peru, and they brought me back this hanging pepper monstrocity. It was like a pepper chandelier, and for a month or two I was picking peppers off and trying them on different things. I should have studied up a bit because I found out later that I was messing with the habañero, and just scorching myself.

If I go all out with my fajitas or tacos and make the salsa and the guacamole, it's quite a bit of slicing and dicing, which I find therapeutic. For my dad, this was one of those easy meals that were quick and tasty. I don't think his interest in the dish is quite the same as mine.

I've continued to tweak my own take on this dish, in hopes of mastering it, because I've had it for a long time, in several different forms, and it keeps popping up in different places in my life journey.

My dad gave me this cast-iron grill. He had cooked on it for the longest time. Then while it was in his shop, a hammer fell on it and the grill grate broke. I knew how much he liked the grill, so I called the company up and asked if they could send a replacement grill grate. It wasn't even 20 bucks. After that, my dad got a bigger grill and sent me on my way with this one.

When I was working on my last record [*Songs I Wrote Before I Knew You*], I ate more bar nuts than fajitas, especially when I was writing the sad bastard songs. Lyrically, that's how it happens for me. It's about the story. Poetry is amazing to me. The melody comes out of the lyrics, out of the feeling.

Fajitas, tacos, and cooking in general create a state of mind that I find healing and therapeutic. My music is subtle and mellow, but I think there's something very real about the human condition that I'm trying to get across. Just by speaking simply about what I see, or what I do, or maybe crafting a story about familiar images. But I think subtlety along with real freshness have to do with both the food and what I like about songwriting. It's a little lame, but there is a comparison to be made. Ladies don't mind it either when you can cook. This is one of those second or third date things. Cook them tacos, and they'll love you forever.

My passion for cooking has taught me the value of subtlety. Subtlety is key, and I didn't realize that for the longest time. Writing a song, 'I have all this I want to say,' but you can shorten the spectrum into this language that still contains the spectrum, but so subtly and eloquently that you no longer have a hundred-ingredient salsa, you just have pico, and it's freaking awesome."

## Grilled Chicken Tacos

### Marinated Chicken

Juice of 1 large lime
2 cloves garlic, minced or crushed
1 teaspoon ground cumin
1 teaspoon cumin seed
1 teaspoon oregano
2 tablespoons olive oil
Salt and pepper to taste
1 pound chicken (thighs, or breasts cut into fingers)

### Green Apple Slaw

1 green apple, thinly sliced
Juice of ½ lime
½ red onion, finely chopped
Small handful cilantro, chopped
½ jalapeño, seeded and thinly sliced
Pinch of salt

Grilled Chicken Tacos with Green Apple Slaw
and Gorgonzola Cream

Andrew Duhon and the Lonesome Crows,
with Jonathan Harris on guitar, at Voodoo

## Gorgonzola Cream

1 small clove garlic
⅓ cup gorgonzola cheese crumbles
1 dollop sour cream
½ teaspoon black pepper, coarsely ground
1 teaspoon lime juice
Salt to taste

Mix marinade ingredients together in a Ziploc bag. Add chicken, close bag, massage chicken, and refrigerate for about 4 hours. Then, for slaw, pour lime juice over apple slices to prevent browning; toss with red onion, cilantro, jalapeño, and salt. Cover with plastic wrap and set aside in the refrigerator.

For gorgonzola cream, simply mix all ingredients together in a bowl.

Grill chicken over charcoal until done and lightly charred, then chop into bite-sized pieces.

Serve in fresh tortillas (don't forget to buy some!), which you heat first, one by one, in a dry skillet, until brown spots appear. Go to town.

## IN THE KITCHEN WITH

# Susan Cowsill

**SUSAN COWSILL CONSIDERS HERSELF THE CRACK CHICKEN QUEEN:** "My mom and dad both came from Cranston, Rhode Island, outside of Providence. Lots of Italian, Portuguese, and Irish Catholic, which is what we are. The meatloafs and the stews and the roasts, that's all Irish. Anything you can put a potato in. The roast was always smaller than all the potatoes.

My mom was the primary cook in my family. Mom food, food mom, mom food. My dad had one thing he did, which was way complicated because there are so many ingredients in it; it's an Italian spaghetti sauce that has chicken, pork, sausage, meatballs, everything in one pot. It was called Bud's sauce, and that was his one and only thing; my mom made everything else. She was the meatloaf queen, the baked chicken queen, pot roast on the stove, which I don't see much anymore, and beef stew. And then there were these two really horrible dishes based around mashed potatoes. One of them was called hamburger gravy, which was just hamburger [meat], flour, butter, salt and pepper, over mashed potatoes. The other horrible item was called cream of salmon, which was canned salmon and milk and butter and salt and pepper, over mashed potatoes. It was a food product where you had to have

**BORN**
1959 in Canton, Ohio

**NEIGHBORHOOD**
Algiers Point

**INSTRUMENTS**
Vocals, guitar, tambourine

**NOTABLE RECORDING**
"Real Life," *Lighthouse,* 2010

**HOLY TRINITY**
Garlic, lemon, olive oil

a glass of milk right next to you. You don't want to taste it and you don't need to chew it. You could always tell when the paycheck was low because there was that cream of salmon crap. And chipped beef; things that go over mashed potatoes that shouldn't.

I make pies. I'm a really good pie maker. Since Katrina, it was a meditation to make pies. We'd be evacuated in somebody's house, and I'd be sitting there on the phone asking somebody something about where we are, and I'd get stone crazy. I got into baking at that point. I got really good at apple pies and not bad at lemon meringue. I make my own crust and the trick is the cold water, and when it goes in. I learned pie crusts from my sister-in-law. Water goes in while it's scootching around in the food processor, and it's all about staring at it to see what consistency it is. If you go too far, pull it out, start over. I use shortening. It's the American way, the Betty Crocker way. Crisco, flour, salt. I like to put a little sugar in.

I got scared about doing this interview because I cook off the top of my head. I don't think about how much I'm putting in. I cook like I write; just throwing it in and hoping it works. The recipe I want to give you is paneed chicken. I don't like deep-fried food, and deep-fried is terrible for you—bless our hearts, literally. I'm primarily olive oil, but I will pop in a little cooking oil, maybe to give it a little more of a crunchy outer coating. And then when I fry the chicken, it's only in an inch or so. I mean, maybe an inch and a half, but then it starts to evaporate.

As I go along, at some point, I have to stop, scoop out all the brown bits because now we're smoking and burning. Clean out the cast iron, start over. If I don't do that the pieces at the end are much darker than the ones in the front. I don't think you can print this, but my kids call it crack chicken. Doesn't that read well? We usually serve it with mashed potatoes and broccoli and bearnaise sauce, which has become the ketchup of our household. You take the Knorr envelope, cup of milk, five pounds of butter and—boom, bearnaise!

And then there's the mac and cheese. It was my mom's, my grandmother's, maybe my great-grandmother's—no, I don't think they made Kraft singles back in great-grandmother's day. Mac is something mom fed us a lot because you can make a giant vat of it and it spreads out among seven children. As a child, I didn't care for it because it had tomato in it, but now I love it. You've got the crunchy cheese on top. Half the family wants it burnt, half of the family doesn't. Strangely, only me and my brother Paul carried the recipe down.

Also, we have Saints Sundays, every game day when we're home we have our friends over. Always the boys from the Glasgow band, Sam and Jack Craft. Even when we're not here they will come, because we've got that big TV we got for Katrina. Katrina's like Christmas sometimes, when you say it like that. 'Oh, we got this for Katrina!' 'What holiday is that?' 'You don't know the Katrina holiday, when everybody got new stuff?' Christmas, Hanukkah and Katrina—I don't know if you can print that either. Everybody brings food. The Craft brothers bring Sambalaya or Jackbalaya, which is jambalaya made by Sam or Jack—whose middle name is Chachere. That's important to mention, that they're Chachere babies. It's in their name. So when they say they'll bring jambalaya, I say 'Okay.'"

Paneed Chicken

Susan Cowsill during sound check at Southport Music Hall

# Paneed Chicken

4 boneless chicken breasts
1 cup Italian bread crumbs
1 handful (about 2 tablespoons) flour
1 tablespoon Italian seasoning
1 teaspoon Tony Chachere's Creole Seasoning
1 teaspoon garlic powder
4 eggs
½ cup milk
1 cup olive oil
½ cup cooking oil

Slice breasts horizontally (if more than 1-inch thick) and pound each piece with a meat tenderizer or upside-down-turned glass to half-an-inch thick. Combine bread crumbs, flour, Italian seasoning, seasoned salt, and garlic powder in a wide bowl. Mix eggs and milk in another wide bowl or baking dish, and soak chicken for 10 minutes. Lift chicken out of egg-milk mixture and coat each piece with bread crumb mixture by pressing each side into crumbs; place on a dry cookie sheet. Heat oil in a large cast-iron frying pan. Fry chicken over medium-high heat (oil should be 325-350 degrees) until golden brown and crispy, about 3 minutes on each side. Serve with Knorr's Bearnaise sauce.

**IN THE KITCHEN WITH**

# DJ Captain Charles

*"I eat my toast, and then I eat the oatmeal."*

**BORN**
1962 in New Orleans, Louisiana

**NEIGHBORHOOD**
Magnolia, Zion City

**INSTRUMENTS**
Controller, laptop, vocals, drums

**HOLY TRINITY**
PET milk, sugar, butter

**DJ CAPTAIN CHARLES TRIES TO KEEP IT SIMPLE:** "I purchased this building in '07, and didn't have a plan what I was going to do with it then. Found out my youngest daughter (Javonda) can cook, 'Let's try and open a little restaurant and see what it'll do.' In the '80s, I had a po-boy shop: Captain Charles' Po-Boys. It was on Washington and Robertson, right by the Magnolia Projects, and then I had a sno-ball stand between all that, in the '80s, '90s.

Somehow I wound back up with another restaurant [Cafe on the Ave, since closed]. Somebody kept saying, 'You know, Javonda is cooking,' and I said, 'Javonda is cooking? Na-huh.' During the Super Bowl week, when the Saints was in the playoffs, I said, 'Let's try some jambalaya,' so she cooked a jambalaya and I enjoyed it. Everybody enjoyed the jambalaya. After that, I was convinced. We have folks who come here and want to order her gumbo. She does a hell of a gumbo, and sometimes folks come in and ask just for the juice.

What do I cook? I can do a po-boy. I can grill steaks. Thursdays we do steaks, so I'm grilling steaks on the deck out there; I grill steaks for lunch every Thursday for 12 o'clock. I'm pretty good. Rare, medium, get a little red in it. I'm pretty good at getting oatmeal together too. That's my favorite dish. By me being in the clubs all night and eating a bunch of junk, either I'm eating chicken or grits or pancakes, and it's not good for you, it's too fatty. So when I get home I put some fiber in me. Every night when I go home, I put some water on the stove, put my oatmeal, let the oatmeal cook. No salt. Real creamy. It's a big bowl and I eat it all. I put butter, cream, and sugar on it. Sometimes I cut up some bananas, but I'm not a raisin person. The only way I can eat raisins is the Raisinets with the chocolate. Only way.

Also, I get my toast. I dip my [buttered] toast in the oatmeal. I eat my toast, and then I eat the oatmeal. Cream, like canned cream, PET milk, the evaporated milk, I put that in my bowl, stir that in with the sugar until it's sweet and juicy. It has to be juicy so I can dip my toast. I allow the butter to melt on top. I tear my toast up and dip it, eat it. Never no leftovers. I make just enough. Ask me how, I couldn't tell you. Luck! But I've been eating oatmeal my whole life; my grandmother introduced me to it and I love it. I might have been three. Coming back in those days and being poor, not having food stamps, if you didn't have nothing else to eat, you'd either eat the oatmeal or the rice and eggs, and that was your meal. Oatmeal, I was raised up on that and I have never gotten away from it. It's something I love doing.

Here, in the morning, folks come in and ask for rice and eggs. Call it a poor man's special. Have you ever tried rice and eggs? Good meal. If you want them scrambled, scramble your eggs. If you want fried, fry. Cook your rice, add a little salt and pepper, and mix it up. Like all the Chinese people do it, we've been doing that for years. That was like our meal. We fed five people off of that. Some people put hot sauce, but I don't eat a lot of hot.

Folks come in here and ask for eggs and rice because not a lot of people sell it.

My vision was, when I decided to do a cafe, make it simple. But people kind of dictate what they want. So we have to give people what they want. 'I want to be able to come in and order some red beans and rice.' Or they'll come in and order some white beans, smothered chicken, or some macaroni and cheese. I did not have that vision of doing a lunch special every day, but we wound up doing that. Steaks on Thursday, seafood on Friday. I wanted to focus more on a cafe; nachos and wi-fi. But when folks started coming, we had to cater to the crowd. I wanted to do more health foods—salads, grilled stuff, baked chicken, but folks rather fried chicken than baked chicken. Tomorrow they'll complain about their weight but today, 'Hey, give me some of that fried chicken!'

We do more better with specials. People like what they like. They love it and they don't try to change it.

My grandma was the cook in the family. She did all the cooking. You got home from school and she used to cook chitlins. I could never eat it. Back in those days, you bought them and you had to clean them yourself. When I got home, the whole house was stinking, it was terrible. Everybody in my house would eat them, I was the only one who didn't. I still don't eat them. I'm a basic person. I like red beans, smothered chops, smothered chicken, candied yams, green peas, creamed corn, or whole corn.

I grew up in the Magnolia. I moved out of the Magnolia and my mother moved us to Zion City, right on the other side of this canal, behind the storage place. We used to play football right here—right here was a toy center, swimming pools. And here on the neutral ground, back in the '70s, there used to be a police talent show, and the inmates used to be the band, and people in the community would come out and perform. There's a lot of history in this area. I have a lot of real estate here. This place used to be a gas station.

It gets on my nerves if I don't have any PET milk when I come home. There was only one Walgreens that's open 24 hours, on St. Charles—the one on Carrollton just opened—and I get home late at night and then run and get my can of PET milk. If I come home at four in the morning and have no milk or no sugar, we have a problem; I have to go get some. So I walk right out the house and get right back in the car at three in the morning. Go get that milk, or get that sugar. Sometime the butter too. For whatever reason, I guess it's a mind thing, oatmeal just don't taste right without that butter."

DJ Captain Charles at the Zulu Ball
Photo by Mookie Square

## Oatmeal

His favorite meal, served with evaporated milk.

½ cup instant oatmeal
1 cup water
4 tablespoons evaporated milk
3 teaspoons sugar
½ tablespoon butter
Buttered toast

Cook oatmeal in a pot, according to directions on box. Do not add salt. Pour oatmeal into a bowl. Stir in evaporated milk and sugar until creamy. Let butter melt on top. Dip toast and eat.

## IN THE KITCHEN WITH

# Martin Krusche

"You dig?"

**BORN**
1965 in Munich, Bavaria, Germany

**NEIGHBORHOOD**
Upper Ninth Ward

**INSTRUMENTS**
Saxophone

**NOTABLE RECORDING**
"Turkey on the Westbank,"
*Aliens of Extraordinary Ability*,
Magnetic Ear, 2010

**HOLY TRINITY**
Ginger, curry, soy sauce

**MARTIN KRUSCHE IS PERFECTLY HARMLESS—TO VITAMINS:** "Let me show you my pot. I fill this one. Magnetic Ear will play every Sunday in January at the AllWays Lounge, and the main selling point is free food at 8 and then we play at 8:30. When we did Live at the Saturn Bar, I wanted to make a live record, and to sweeten the pot for everybody, I cooked. That's the idea; make the band happy and the audience, and see how much of a draw can you get. Not charging anything—not at the door, not for the food—just make them tip. Sometimes, that way you get more money than if you ask for five bucks at the door. They feel like, 'I already paid.' But if they come and everything's for free and they really dig it, they go like, 'Let's put down 10 bucks. This is awesome.' We're all in a low yield something.

I started cooking Indian when I was living in Cologne, Germany, in 1992. There was an Indian restaurant that had dal and it was so good that I got totally addicted to it, but it was also so expensive that I needed to learn how to cook it myself.

I make a curry paste as my base, and then you can go any direction from there. If I have three different dishes—chicken curry, maybe Massaman with the peanut sauce, vegetable curry and dal—they all come from the same curry paste that I made, but I give every one of those dishes a slightly different flavor. For example, in dal I put extra cumin and cardamom. Once you have your curry paste, the rest is just like regular cooking. You can play with all of this.

The onion, garlic, and ginger is very finely minced. Throw that in super hot oil, and be careful not to burn it—you've got to be totally on top of it—and then pile the curry powder on. That's how you get your curry paste. But I also use this for Italian bolognese sauce. I throw ginger in everything because I'm a ginger freak. For the bolognese sauce, you don't have to super-fine mince the onion, garlic, and ginger, you just chop them roughly— and carrots! I use carrots too. Again, hot oil in the pan and throw all this in, and you start cooking it on the outside, but don't totally cook it. Now, throw it in the blender and the fresh and uncooked mixes with the cooked and slightly oily outside and you have a second flavor explosion. You dig? Now you have this orange sauce and the meat that you already fried on the side and mix that together and let that simmer for as long as you can stand it. All the carrots bring a lot of sugar and it's so good. I don't care if it's original Italian.

When I take the stuff into the blender it goes together with the whole tomatoes from the can, with the juice, all of it. Tomatoes in the can often are better than fresh tomatoes from the store because they take the ripe ones where they don't have to worry about the transportation and sometimes you get really good tomatoes in the can. I used to bother with fresh tomatoes, scalding them in boiling water, and it's not worth the work.

These are my water bottles. I buy the gallon jugs and I fill them right away into glass bottles so they don't take on any more plastic taste. I'm shopping for the most recently filled Kentwood. It's all about the dates.

I do my vegetable shopping at Bubba's Produce Co. I go once a week and spend about $20. You get a pound of garlic for $1.20 while you pay $6 in the supermarket. And it's huge! I always get zucchini, carrots, bell peppers, snap beans, onions, garlic, ginger, all this stuff. Plenty, always. They have crazy early hours, like five in the morning and you can walk in there until noon. Walk into the office and give them your order, and they get it together for you. You get so much produce for your money, you can't beat it.

The wok is hip because the oil gathers at the bottom where you need it. Plus it helps to cook vegetables and not overcook them. It's all about heat. As long as the vegetable retains color, the vitamins are unharmed."

## Vegetable Curry

(Serves a whole band.)

1 root fresh ginger, cut into chunks
2 medium onions, roughly diced
6 large cloves garlic
½ cup peanut oil
½ cup Indian curry powder
4 large carrots, cut into 1-inch strips
1 pound green beans, in 1-inch pieces
2 yellow bell peppers, diced
2 red bell peppers, diced
4 zucchini, cut into 1-inch logs
3 small beef bouillon cubes, dissolved in a little hot
    water

Vegetable Curry

Martin Krusche plays with Joe Cabral and Jason Jurzak
as Magnetic Ear, at Maison, on Frenchmen Street

2 tablespoons raw sugar

1 tablespoon ground coriander

1 teaspoon ground cardamom

2 tablespoons turmeric

1 cup plain yogurt

¼ cup sour cream

½ cup creamy peanut butter

1 package firm tofu, cut into cubes

¼ cup peanut oil

Finely mince ginger, onion, and garlic in a food processor.
Fry in hot oil to make a paste. Season with curry powder.

Set aside. Bring 1 cup of water to a boil and cook/steam
carrots and green beans until slightly softened. Drain and
set aside. Fry bell peppers for a couple of minutes, add
carrots and green beans, then zucchini. Add curry paste.
Season with bouillon cubes, sugar, coriander, cardamom,
and turmeric. Add yogurt, sour cream, and peanut butter.
Salt to taste. Fry tofu separately in oil, then add to curry.
Stir carefully. Serve with basmati rice.

**IN THE KITCHEN WITH**

# Charmaine Neville

**BORN**
1956 in New Orleans, Louisiana

**NEIGHBORHOOD**
Lower Ninth Ward

**INSTRUMENTS**
Vocals, percussion, drums

**NOTABLE RECORDING**
"Up Up Up," *Up Up Up*, 1996

**HOLY TRINITY**
Bell pepper, onion, garlic

**CHARMAINE NEVILLE WOULD LIKE YOU TO CALL HER IF YOU CAN MAKE HER A DRESS OUT OF CHOCOLATE:** "You know, we have a law in Louisiana. If you live here and you can't cook, we make you move. That's just written law. The way I learned how to cook was from everybody. I learned things from the Jewish lady around the corner, the Irish lady down the street, the Italian lady in the next block, the Vietnamese lady, the Brazilian lady, the German lady. You learn from everybody. You know what's going to be on the menu every day of the week, but you also know that even though your mama is cooking red beans and rice and the Italian lady across the street is cooking red beans and rice, hers is going to taste different, so you go by her house. Everybody makes spaghetti sauce, but it's going to taste different. This person might do just tomatoes, ground meat, and seasonings; that person might do chicken and eggs!

Everybody had a day of the week to cook for the family and I was eight when I did my first meal. I lived with my great aunt, it was during the summertime and we were somewhere in Mississippi, not far from Jackson. It was all kids, because your parents leave you in the summertime with somebody in the country. My sisters, my cousins, the neighbors! That day I had to catch a chicken, wring his neck, pluck him, cut him up, batter him, fry him, make macaroni and cheese—I cooked greens, I made cornbread. As a matter of fact, it was strawberry cornbread. What else did we have? Well, gravy and mashed potatoes, and she might have showed me how to fry okra that day too, so that was the meal that day.

Strawberry cornbread. I've been making it my whole life, and you make it easily. You make your regular cornbread and you take your strawberries and wash them and slice them and fold them into the batter so the bread does not get pink. You want the regular color cornbread but you want the strawberry slices to be throughout it. You don't want pink bread.

I love to feed people. After Katrina, on Fridays, I had the fish fries in my backyard. Nobody had kitchens, and the first thing I did was I got my kitchen together. When people had money, I asked for a donation, and that helped someone get floors for their house, or get an electrician to come, or get a moving van, buy rugs, whatever. I had people come help me too. One lady made this great, great tea and she would come all the way from across the lake and bring tea every Friday. Another friend of mine from down in Chalmette would bring salads. Cooking and feeding the community helped me a whole lot. It made me feel normal.

I always wanted to have a restaurant where all I did was make people feel good. [For a while, I had] a spot on St. Charles Avenue, on top of the St. Charles Tavern. I was the waitress, the cashier, the bouncer, the dishwasher, and the cook. I was making deep-dish apple pie with three crusts, triple-chocolate bread pudding, and of course regular New Orleans bread pudding—my daddy told me, 'Look,

you've got to have real bread pudding! I don't want this chocolate stuff!'—butter pecan pound cake, your mama's jelly cake, banana pudding, strawberry cornbread, sweet potato pecan pie, lemon squares, lemon-lime velvet cake, rum cakes, 7-Up cakes, better-than-sex cakes—normal and ordinary New Orleans desserts. Mrs. Katz, this lady who used to live around the corner from me made an apple butter cake, so—of course—I got her recipe. All of my recipes come from different neighborhood people.

My kids grew up with, 'If you don't eat all your dessert, you go to bed without dinner.' I love desserts and I'm the quintessential chocoholic. I always wanted to do an ad for some candy store where I'd make a dress out of chocolate, with a bite out of it! I've dreamt of that for a long time. Some candy company, call me!"

## Chocolate Strawberry Short Cake

"I love strawberry short cake, so why not make a chocolate strawberry short cake?"

4 ounces chocolate, chopped
⅓ cup unsweetened cocoa
1 cup boiling water
2¼ cups flour
2 teaspoons baking powder
1 teaspoon baking soda
¼ teaspoon sea salt
2 sticks unsalted butter
2 cups sugar
3 large eggs
2 teaspoons vanilla extract

Chocolate Berry Short Cake
(when you can't get strawberries...)

Charmaine Neville at Snug Harbor

1 cup milk
2 cups strawberries, sliced
1 pint heavy whipping cream

Grease two 8" round baking pans, and preheat oven to 350 degrees. Pour boiling water over chopped chocolate and cocoa. Stir until melted. In a separate bowl, whisk flour, baking powder, baking soda, and salt together. In another bowl, beat butter and sugar until smooth; add eggs one at a time; add vanilla. When chocolate mixture is cool, mix everything together, adding milk. Pour batter into baking pans and bake for about 40 minutes. Cool.

Whip cream. Mix strawberries with about a third of the cream and place between layers. Cover cake with remaining cream. Enjoy with a tall glass of cold milk.

IN THE KITCHEN WITH

# Dancing Man 504

**DANCING MAN 504 LEARNED FROM HIS MOTHER THAT IT TAKES BALLS TO MAKE THE BEST RED BEANS:** "Cajun red beans have always been my favorite, so that's what I'm cooking today. It has the hot sausage balls in it; it's my mom's secret. You have to cut the hot sausage links open, take out the filling, and roll the meat into small balls, and you wait until your beans are creamy, and that's when you throw the hot sausage balls in—to add that spice. You don't have to use Zatarain's, or hot sauce. You still get that hotness that you're looking for. A lady told me that the definition of Cajun beans is that it has andouille sausage in it, which is a sausage made in southern Louisiana. But the smoked sausage, the Double D, was made in the Lower Ninth Ward, so we'd take that over the andouille because that's our neighborhood meat. So we made it Ninth Ward Cajun.

My mother was from Franklinton, Louisiana. She would cook things like duck, rabbit, and deer. But then for me, she'd cook baked chicken, or pork and beans and wieners. I'm a big fan of that. It's quick and fast and easy. And she made the best gumbo ever. I'll tell you my mother's gumbo secret: when she added the water, she'd take some boiled crabs and add that in for the flavor, and then take

*"When my beans come to creaminess, I add some more beans."*

**BORN**
1967 in New Orleans, Louisiana

**NEIGHBORHOOD**
Ninth Ward

**INSTRUMENTS**
Feet, flute

**NOTABLE RECORDING**
"Dancing Man 504 in the Rain," *YouTube*

**HOLY TRINITY**
Zatarain's Creole Mustard, black pepper, celery

those out and put in the raw crabs to grab everything. I try to use that in my cooking—don't follow the recipe, but to follow what I'm after.

I grew up over by Kentucky and Rampart. You wouldn't go over the bridge; you'd go on the side and turn right. In the morning, the train would pass and you'd hear the soldiers at the Navy support center right there on Poland, doing their morning runs and jogs and singing their songs, and my mom would be cooking breakfast. I come from a family of six—I'm the baby—and we had nieces and nephews and neighbors over, doing a lot of eating and cooking. That's why I'm shocked that I'm not a cook, but a dancer.

Being born in Franklinton, my mom would always say, 'I'm a country girl.' She would cook everything from scratch, that's what she said. But in New Orleans, when we say 'cook from scratch,' what we mean is 'what am I going to cook today?' [scratching head]. That's cooking from scratch. My mother was taught by her mother, and my grandmother was of the Choctaw nation. My mother was real good with growing her own spices and seasonings. I grew up doing a lot of farm work. I'm a city boy, but she would have us picking tomatoes, picking mandarins, and she would grow the cabbage, the lettuce, the okra—I didn't have to pick the okra because it made my hand balloon and turn into a big ball—so I picked mandarins and tangerines. And we'd have misbelief trees. Japanese plums, we call them misbeliefs, because we just can't believe they grow right here! In the Ninth Ward, we had the gardens. Even in St. Bernard Parish, where my father was from, the land off of the railroad tracks, we'd go till the land, and that's where I first learned to drive, out in the field. My dad said I couldn't drive his car in the street,

so I drove it in the dirt. We even grew corn. My mother had a green thumb. She'd say she could grow anything but money. It just won't grow in New Orleans for some reason.

These beans, I cook them exactly like my mother would have done them. The water I soak my beans in is the water that goes on the fire. To me, it's because they've grown a friendship. They trust one another. The water didn't leave the pot, and the beans didn't jump out. When the beans get soft, my mother didn't smash the beans; she'd add a little butter and take the spoon and turn it, and that's what makes them creamy. Otherwise, you lose the beans. I'm a guy who likes texture. I don't want no soupy beans. I want to know that I'm actually eating beans.

I also re-add seasonings when the excess water cooks off and it's getting into that tight gravy. That's when you lock it. In the beginning, to get the beans started, I put seasonings in the water, and then later, I hit it a little more. Then I do a dance in between. My mom would put the beans on a low fire and look at *The Young and the Restless*, *The Guiding Light*, *As the World Turns*. You can't rush your beans; beans are not cooked in one hour. She said three hours to cook your beans. And when my beans come to creaminess, I add some more beans."

## Red Beans with Hot Sausage Balls

1 pound red kidney beans
1 large onion, diced
2-3 stalks celery, diced
1 green bell pepper, diced
4 cloves garlic, minced

Red Beans with Hot Sausage Balls

Dancing Man 504 at French Quarter Fest

2 bay leaves

1 pound Double D hot smoked sausage, cut into slices and then in halves

1 pound fresh hot sausage from Rouses, remove cases and roll into 1-inch balls

1 tablespoon butter

Salt and black pepper to taste

Rinse beans and soak overnight in water in a pot, covering beans with at least 2 inches of water. In the morning, remove about 1 cup of beans from the pot and set aside. Chop and mix onion, celery, bell pepper, and garlic together, adding about half of this mix to beans in the pot. Add bay leaves and simmer, covered, for 1 hour until the beans begin to soften. Add reserved beans, the rest of the onion mix, along with the sliced smoked sausage. Cover and simmer for 1½ hours until the beans that were added last are soft enough to eat. Stir in butter and drop in the hot sausage balls. Simmer for another 30 minutes. Add salt and black pepper to taste and serve over rice.

# P.S.

The reason I'm so excited about this book is because music is imparted. It's multi-generational, it's passed down, and part of the music tradition is a lot of food being consumed and talked about. There is a lot of food talk on the buses when the musicians go on the road to make a living. So many of the conversations I've heard are about: "Boy, do I miss those smothered pork chops." It's those talks all the time that are part of the music culture, and it's not just the funeral where the repast food is always awesome, but it's the backstage area, where the producer might have horrible finger sandwiches and just the regular yucky food, but if there are a lot of New Orleans musicians, somebody has made a platter of deviled eggs, or some crawfish dip—and that's not their job to cater, but they're going to show up with some little goodie that somebody made, or maybe they made. When you look at Facebook, the majority of people who are posting what they're eating, drinking, and cooking are musicians, because they have time on their hands. I'm not saying musicians don't work hard, but a lot of them have to have a wife with a day job, so they're sitting at home making grandmother's smothered chicken, and they know when so-and-so is on sale at the Breaux Mart. Musicians go: "Hey, did you know they have brisket on sale?"

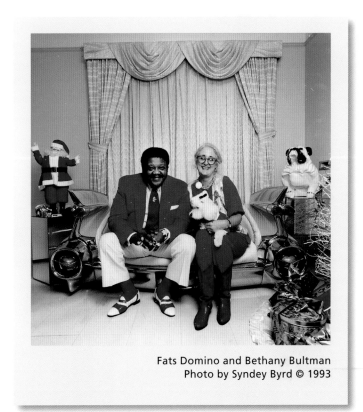

Fats Domino and Bethany Bultman
Photo by Syndey Byrd © 1993

Fats Domino always brought pots and pans and ingredients from Louisiana when he went on the road, and cooked for his band the entire time. He didn't want anyone getting sick, and we're people who really like our own flavors. He said, "If I cook it myself, I know what it is." So that's what he did. Fats, before the gig, was making that food.

Fats made this hogshead cheese that was the spiciest thing I have ever eaten. I swear, I thought blood was going to come out of my palms, it was just so hot. He served that with homemade strawberry wine so incredibly sweet it was like hummingbird food.

—*Bethany Bultman*

# Recipe Index